SHIRLEY COLE-HARDING

Recent Issues
in the Analysis
of Behavior

Recent Issues in the Analysis of Behavior

B. F. SKINNER

Merrill Publishing Company
A Bell & Howell Company
Columbus   Toronto   London   Melbourne

Published by Merrill Publishing Company
A Bell & Howell Information Company
Columbus, Ohio 43216

This book was set in Palatino.

Administrative Editor: Vicki Knight
Production Coordinator: Sharon Rudd
Cover Designer: Brian Deep
Text Designer: Cynthia Brunk

Library of Congress Catalog Card Number: 88–63288
International Standard Book Number: 0–675–20674–X
Printed in the United States of America
1 2 3 4 5 6 7 8 9—92 91 90 89

To all behavior analysts

Preface

This is the fifth in a series of collections of papers. The first was called *Cumulative Record* (Skinner, 1959; third edition, 1972). It contained papers published over a period of almost 40 years. The papers in the second, *Contingencies of Reinforcement, a theoretical analysis* (Skinner, 1969), were published in the 1960s. Those in the third, *Reflections on Behaviorism and Society* (Skinner, 1978), and fourth, *Upon Further Reflection* (Skinner, 1987), showed a narrowing of range and a concentration on the practices and implications of a behavioral analysis. Most of the present volume is devoted to theoretical and professional issues and is written primarily for psychologists and behavior analysts. Like the other four volumes there is necessarily some repetition, and like them the chapters can be read in any order.

I am indebted to Margaret Vaughan, Julie Vargas, and Evalyn Segal for their useful criticism.

Acknowledgments

Chapters in this book were originally published in the following places. Permission to reprint is gratefully acknowledged.

Chapter 1: *London Times Literary Supplement*. (May 8, 1987).

Chapter 2: Skinner, B. F. (in press). The origins of cognitive thought. *American Psychologist*. Copyright 1989 by the American Psychological Association. Adapted by permission of the publisher.

Chapter 3: *Thinking Clearly About Psychology: Essays in Honor of Paul E. Meehl.* (in press). D. Cicchetti & W. Grove (Eds.). Minneapolis: University of Minnesota Press.

Chapter 4: *Rule-Governed Behavior: Cognition, Contingencies, and Instructional Control.* (1988). Hayes, S. E. (Ed.). New York: Plenum.

Chapter 5: *Evolution of Social Behavior and Integrative Levels.* (1988). Gary Greenberg & Ethel Tobach (Eds.). Hillsdale, NJ: Lawrence Erlbaum Associates.

Chapter 6: Skinner, B. F. (1987). Whatever happened to psychology as the science of behavior? *American Psychologist*, 42(8), 1–7. Copyright 1987 by the American Psychological Association. Adapted by permission of the publisher.

Chapter 7: *Journal of Behavior Therapy and Experimental Psychiatry.* (1988).

Chapter 9: *Phi Delta Kappan.* (October 1986).

Chapter 10: *Journal of the History of the Behavioral Sciences.* (1987).

Chapter 11: *Beyond Freedom and Dignity.* (1988). B. F. Skinner. London: Penguin Books, Ltd.

Contents

◆ PART ONE ◆

Theoretical Issues

◆ CHAPTER 1 ◆

The Place of Feeling in the Analysis of Behavior

A review of Gerald Zuriff's *Behaviorism: A Conceptual Reconstruction* (1985) in the *London Times Literary Supplement* (1985) begins with a story about two behaviorists. They make love, and then one of them says, "That was fine for you. How was it for me?" The reviewer, P. N. Johnson-Laird, insists that there is a "verisimilitude" with behaviorist theory. Behaviorists are not supposed to have feelings, or at least to admit that they have them. Of the many ways in which behaviorism has been misunderstood for so many years, that is perhaps the commonest.

A possibly excessive concern for "objectivity" may have caused the trouble. Methodological behaviorists, like logical positivists, argued that science must confine itself to events that can be observed by two or more people; truth must be truth by agreement. What one sees through introspection does not qualify. There is a private world of feelings and states of mind, but it is out of reach of a second person and hence of science. That was not a very satisfactory position, of course. How people feel is often as important as what they do.

Radical behaviorism has never taken that line. Feeling is a kind of sensory action, like seeing or hearing. We see a tweed jacket, for example, and we also feel it. That is not quite like feeling depressed, of course. We know something about the organs with which we feel the jacket but little, if anything, about those with which we feel depressed. We can also feel *of* the jacket by running our fingers over the cloth to increase the stimulation, but there does not seem to be any way to feel *of* depression. We have other ways of sensing the jacket, and we do various things with it. In other words, we have other ways of knowing what we are feeling. But what are we feeling when we feel depressed?

3

Theoretical Issues

William James anticipated the behaviorist's answer: what we feel is a condition of our body. We do not cry because we are sad, said James, we are sad because we cry. That was fudging a little, of course, because we do much more than cry when we feel sad, and we can feel sad when we are not crying, but it was pointing in the right direction: what we feel is bodily conditions. Physiologists will eventually observe them in another way, as they observe any other part of the body. Walter B. Cannon's *Bodily Changes in Pain, Hunger, Fear, and Rage* (1929) was an early study of a few conditions often felt. Meanwhile, we ourselves can respond to them directly. We do so in two different ways. For example, we respond to stimuli from our joints and muscles in one way when we move about and in a different way when we say that we feel relaxed or lame. We respond to an empty stomach in one way when we eat and in a different way when we say that we are hungry.

The verbal responses in those examples are the products of special contingencies of reinforcement. They are arranged by listeners, and they are especially hard to arrange when what is being talked about is out of the listener's reach, as it usually is when it is within the speaker's skin. The very privacy which suggests that we ought to know our own bodies especially well is a severe handicap for those who must teach us to know them. We can teach a child to name an object, for example, by presenting or pointing to the object, pronouncing its name, and reinforcing a similar response by the child, but we cannot do that with a bodily state. We cannot present or point to a pain, for example. Instead, we infer the presence of the pain from some public accompaniment. We may see the child take a hard fall, for example, and say, "That must have hurt," or we see the child wince and ask, "Does something hurt?" We can respond only to the blow or the wince, but the child also feels a private stimulus and may say "hurt" when it occurs again without a public accompaniment. Since public and private events seldom coincide exactly, words for feelings have never been taught as successfully as words for objects. Perhaps that is why philosophers and psychologists so seldom agree when talking about feelings and states of mind, and why there is no acceptable science of feeling.

For centuries, of course, it has been said that we behave in given ways because of our feelings. We eat because we feel hungry, strike because we feel angry, and in general do what we feel like doing. If that were true, our faulty knowledge of feelings would be disastrous. No science of behavior would be possible. But what is felt is not an initial or initiating cause. William James was quite wrong about his "becauses." We do not cry *because* we are sad or feel sad *because* we cry; we cry *and* feel sad because something has happened. (Perhaps someone we loved has died.) It is easy to mistake what we feel as a cause because we feel it while we are behaving (or even before we behave), but the events which are actually responsible for what we do (and hence what we feel) lie in the possibly distant past. The experimental analysis of behavior advances our understanding of feelings by clarifying the roles of both past and present environments. Here are three examples.

LOVE

A critic has said that, for a behaviorist, "I love you" means "You reinforce me." Good behaviorists would say, "You reinforce my behavior" rather than "You reinforce me," because it is behavior, not the behaving person, that is being reinforced in the sense of being strengthened; but they would say much more. There is no doubt a reinforcing element in loving. Everything lovers do that brings them closer together or keeps them from being separated is reinforced by those consequences, and that is why they spend as much time together as they can. We describe the private effect of a reinforcer when we say that it "pleases us" or "makes us feel good," and in that sense "I love you" means "You please me or make me feel good." But the contingencies responsible for what is felt must be analyzed further.

The Greeks had three words for love, and they are still useful. Mentalistic psychologists may try to distinguish among them by looking at how love feels but much more can be learned from the relevant contingencies of selection, both natural selection and operant reinforcement. *Eros* is usually taken to mean sexual love, in part no doubt because the word *erotic* is derived from it. It is that part of making love that is due to natural selection; we share it with other species. (Many forms of parental love are also due to natural selection and are also examples of *eros*. To call mother love erotic is not to call it sexual.) Erotic lovemaking may also be modified by operant conditioning, but a genetic connection survives, because the susceptibility to reinforcement by sexual contact is an evolved trait. (Variations which have made individuals more susceptible have increased their sexual activity and hence their contribution to the future of the species.) In most other species the genetic tendency is the stronger. Courtship rituals and modes of copulation vary little from individual to individual and are usually related to optimal times of conception and seasons for the bearing of offspring. In *homo sapiens* sexual reinforcement predominates and yields a much greater frequency and variety of lovemaking.

Philia refers to a different kind of reinforcing consequence and, hence, a different state to be felt and called love. The root *phil* appears in words like *philosophy* (love of wisdom) and *philately* (love of postage stamps), but other things are loved in that way when the root word is not used. People say they "love Brahms" when they are inclined to listen to his works—perform them, perhaps, or go to concerts where they are performed, or play recordings. People who "love Renoir" tend to go to exhibitions of his paintings or buy them (alas, usually copies of them) to be looked at. People who "love Dickens" tend to acquire and read his books. We say the same thing about places ("I love Venice"), subject matters ("I love astronomy"), characters in fiction ("I love Daisy Miller"), kinds of people ("I love children"), and, of course, friends in whom we have no erotic interest. (It is sometimes hard to distinguish between *eros* and *philia*. Those who "love Brahms" may report that they play or listen to his works almost erotically, and courtship and lovemaking are sometimes practiced as forms of art.)

If we can say that *eros* is primarily a matter of natural selection and *philia* of operant conditioning, then *agape* represents a third process of selection—cultural evolution. *Agape* comes from a word meaning to welcome or, as a dictionary puts it, "receive gladly." By showing that we are pleased when another person joins us, we reinforce joining. The direction of reinforcement is reversed. It is not our behavior but the behavior of those we love that is reinforced. The principle effect is on the group. By showing that we are pleased by what other people do, we reinforce the doing and thus strengthen the group.

The direction of reinforcement is also reversed in *eros* if the manner in which we make love is affected by signs that our lover is pleased. It is also reversed in *philia* when our love for Brahms, for example, takes the form of founding or joining a society for the promotion of his works, or when we show our love for Venice by contributing to a fund to preserve the city. We also show a kind of *agape* when we honor heroes, leaders, scientists, and others from whose achievement we have profited. We are said to "worship" them in the etymological sense of proclaiming their worth. (When we say that we venerate them the *ven* is from the Latin *venus*, which meant any kind of pleasing thing.) *Worship* is the commoner word when speaking of the love of god, for which the New Testament used *agape*.

A reversed direction of reinforcement must be explained, especially when it calls for sacrifice. We may act to please a lover because our own pleasure is then increased, but why should we do so when it is not? We may promote the works of Brahms or help save Venice because we then have more opportunities to enjoy them, but why should we do so when that is not the case? The primary reinforcing consequences of *agape* are, in fact, artificial. They are contrived by our culture and contrived, moreover, just because the kind of thing we then do has helped the culture solve its problems and survive.

ANXIETY

Very different states of the body are generated by aversive stimuli, and they are felt in different ways. Many years ago W. K. Estes and I were rash enough to report an experiment under the title "Some quantitative properties of anxiety" (1941) although we were writing about rats. A hungry rat pressed a lever at a low, steady rate, under intermittent reinforcement with bits of food. Once or twice during an hour-long session, we sounded a tone for three minutes and then lightly shocked the rat through its feet. At first neither the tone nor the shock had any marked effect on the rate of responding, but the rat soon began to respond more slowly while the tone was sounding and eventually stopped altogether. Under rather similar circumstances a person might say, "I stopped what I was doing because I felt anxious."

In that experiment, the disrupted behavior was produced by intermittent operant reinforcement, but the disruption would usually be attributed to respondent (classical or Pavlovian) conditioning. There is a problem, however. A change in probability of responding or rate of responding is not properly called a response. Moreover, since the shock itself did not suppress responding, there was no substitution of stimuli. The reduced rate seems, paradoxically, to be the innate effect of a necessarily conditioned stimulus.

A paraphrased comment of Freud's begins as follows: "A person experiences anxiety in a situation of danger and helplessness." A "situation of danger" is a situation that resembles one in which painful things have happened. Our rat was in a situation of danger while the tone was sounding. It was "helpless" in the sense that it could do nothing to stop the tone or escape. The state of its body was presumably similar to the state a person would feel as anxiety, although the verbal contingencies needed for a response comparable to "I feel anxious" were lacking.

The paraphrase of Freud continues: "If the situation threatens to recur in later life, the person experiences anxiety as a signal of impending danger." (It would be better to say "impending harm," because what threatens to recur is the aversive event—the shock for the rat and perhaps something like an automobile accident for the person, but what actually recurs is the condition that preceded that event—the tone, or, say, riding with a reckless driver.) The quotation makes the point that the condition felt as anxiety begins to act as a second conditioned aversive stimulus. As soon as the tone began to generate a particular state of the rat's body, the state itself stood in the same relation to the shock as the tone, and it should have begun to have the same effect. Anxiety thus becomes self-perpetuating and even self-intensifying. A person might say, "I feel anxious, and something terrible always happens when I feel that way," but the contingencies yield a better analysis than any report of how self-perpetuated anxiety feels.

FEAR

A different result would have followed in our experiment if the shock had been contingent upon a response—in other words, if pressing had been punished. The rat would also have stopped pressing, but the bodily state would have been different. It would probably have been called fear. Anxiety is perhaps a kind of fear (we would say that the rat was "afraid another shock would follow"), but that is different from being "afraid to press the lever" because the shock would follow. A difference in the contingencies is unmistakable.

Young behaviorists sometimes contribute an example of fear, relevant here, when they find themselves saying that something pleases them or makes them angry and are embarrassed for having said it. The etymology of the word *embarrassment* as a kind of fear is significant. The root is *bar*, and young behaviorists find themselves barred from speaking freely about their feelings because those who have misunderstood behaviorism have ridiculed them when they have done so. An analysis of how embarrassment feels, made without alluding to antecedents or consequences, would be difficult if not impossible, but the contingencies are clear enough. In general, the more subtle the state felt, the greater the advantage in turning to the contingencies.

Such an analysis has an important bearing on two practical questions: how much can we ever know about what another person is feeling, and how can what is felt be changed? It is not enough to ask other people how or what they feel, because the words they will use in telling us were acquired, as we have seen, from people who did not quite know what they were talking about. Something of the sort seems to have been true of the first use of words to describe private states. The first person who said, "I'm worried" borrowed a word meaning "choked" or "strangled." (*Anger, anguish,* and *anxiety* also come from another word that meant "choked.") But how much like the effect of choking was the bodily state the word was used to describe? All words for feelings seem to have begun as metaphors, and it is significant that the transfer has always been from public to private. No word seems to have originated as the name of a feeling.

The Place of Feeling in the Analysis of Behavior

We do not need to use the names of feelings if we can go directly to the public events. Instead if saying, "I was angry," we can say, "I could have struck him." What was felt was an inclination to strike rather than striking, but the private stimuli must have been much the same. Another way to report what we feel is to describe a setting that is likely to generate the condition felt. After reading Chapman's translation of Homer for the first time, Keats reported that he felt "like some watcher of the skies/ When a new planet swims into his ken." It was easier for his readers to feel what an astronomer would feel upon discovering a new planet than what Keats felt upon reading the book.

It is sometimes said that we can make direct contact with what other people feel through sympathy or empathy. Sympathy seems to be reserved for painful feelings; we sympathize with a person who has lost a fortune but not with one who has made one. When we empathize, we are said to project our feelings into another person, but we cannot actually be moving feelings about, because we also project them into things—when, for example, we commit the pathetic fallacy. What we feel of Lear's rage is not quite what we feel in a raging storm. Sympathy and empathy seem to be effects of imitation. For genetic or personal reasons we tend to do what other people are doing and we may then have similar bodily states to feel. When we do what other *things* are doing, it is not likely that we are sharing feelings.

Sympathy and empathy cannot tell us exactly what a person feels, because part of what is felt depends upon the setting in which the behavior occurs, and that is usually missing in imitation. When lysergic acid diethylamide first attracted attention, psychiatrists were urged to take it to see what it felt like to be psychotic, but acting like a psychotic because one has taken a drug may not create the condition felt by those who are psychotic for other reasons.

That we know what other people feel only when we behave as they behave is clear when we speak of knowing what members of other species feel. Presumably we are more likely to avoid hurting animals if what they would do resembles what we would do when hurt in the same way. That is why we are more likely to hurt the kinds of animals—fish, snakes and insects, for example—which do not behave very much as we do. It is a rare person, indeed, who would not hurt a fly.

To emphasize what is felt rather than the feeling is important when we want to change feelings. Drugs, of course, are often used for that purpose. Some of them (aspirin, for example) break the connection with what is felt. Others create states that appear to compete with or mask troublesome states. According to American television commercials, alcohol yields the good fellowship of *agape* and banishes care. But these are temporary measures, and their effects are necessarily imperfect simulations of what is naturally felt in daily life because the natural settings are lacking.

Feelings are most easily changed by changing the settings responsible for what is felt. We could have relieved the anxiety of our rat by turning off the tone. When a setting cannot be changed, a new history of reinforcement may change its effect. In his remarkable book, *Émile*, Rousseau described what is now called desensitization. If a baby is frightened when plunged into cold water (presumably an innate response), begin with warm water and reduce the temperature a degree a day. The baby will not be frightened when the water is finally cold. Something of the sort could also be done, said Rousseau, with social reactions. If a child is frightened by a person wearing a threatening mask, begin with a friendly one and change it slightly day by day until it becomes threatening, when it will not be frightening.

Psychoanalysis is largely concerned with discovering and changing feelings. An analysis sometimes seems to work by extinguishing the effects of old punishments. When the patient discovers that obscene, blasphemous, or aggressive behavior is tolerated, the therapist emerges as a non-punitive audience. Behavior "repressed" by former punishments then begins to appear. It "becomes conscious" simply in the sense that it begins to be felt. The once offending behavior is not punished, but it is also not reinforced, and it eventually undergoes extinction, a less troublesome method of eradication than punishment.

Cognitive psychologists are among those who most often criticize behaviorism for neglecting feelings, but they themselves have done very little in the field. The computer is not a helpful model. Cognitive psychologists specialize in the behavior of speakers and listeners. Instead of arranging contingencies of reinforcements, they often simply describe them. Instead of observing what their subjects do, they often simply ask them what they would probably do. But the kinds of behavior most often associated with feelings are not easily brought under verbal control. "Cheer up" or "Have a good time" seldom works. Only operant behavior can be executed in response to advice, but if it occurs only for that reason, it has the same shortcomings as imitative behavior. Advice must be taken and reinforcing consequences must follow before the bodily condition that is the intended effect of the advice will be felt. If consequences do not immediately follow, the advice ceases to be taken or the behavior remains nothing more than taking advice.

Fortunately, not everything we feel is troublesome. We enjoy many states of our bodies and, because they are positively reinforcing, do what is needed to produce them. We read books and watch television and, to the extent that we then tend to behave as the characters behave, we feel and possibly enjoy relevant bodily states. Drugs are taken for positively reinforcing effects (but the reinforcement is negative when they are taken primarily to relieve withdrawal symptoms). Religious mystics cultivate special bodily states—by fasting, remaining still or silent, reciting mantras, and so on. Dedicated joggers often report a jogging high.

To confine an analysis of feelings to what is felt may seem to neglect an essential question what is *feeling*, simply as such? We can ask a similar question about any sensory process—for example, what is *seeing*? Philosophers and cognitive psychologists avoid that question by contending that to see something is to make some kind of copy—a "representation," to use the current word. But making a copy cannot be seeing, because the copy must in turn be seen. Nor is it enough, of course, to say simply that seeing is behaving; it is only part of behaving. It is "behaving up to the point of acting." Unfortunately, what happens up to that point is out of reach of the instruments and methods of the behavior analyst and must be left to the physiologist. What remains for the analyst are the contingencies of reinforcement under which things come to be seen and the verbal contingencies under which they come to be described. In the case of feeling, both the conditions felt and what is done in feeling them must be left to the physiologist. What remain for the behavior analyst are the genetic and personal histories responsible for the bodily conditions the physiologist will find.

There are many good reasons why people talk about their feelings. What they say is often a useful indication of what has happened to them or of what they may do. On the point of offering a friend a glass of water, we do not ask, "How long has it been since you last drank any water?" or "If I offer you a glass of water, what are the chances you will accept it?" We ask, "Are you thirsty?" The answer tells us all we need to know. In an experimental analysis, however, we need a better account of the conditions that affect hydration and a better measure of the probability that a subject will drink. A report of how thirsty the subject feels will not suffice.

For at least 3,000 years, however, philosophers, joined recently by psychologists, have looked within themselves for the causes of their behavior. For reasons which are becoming clear, they have never agreed upon what they have found. Physiologists, and especially neurologists, look at the same body in a different and potentially successful way, but even when they have seen it more clearly, they will not have seen initiating causes of behavior. What they will see must in turn be explained either by ethologists, who look for explanations in the evolution of the species, or by behavior analysts, who look at the histories of individuals. The inspection or introspection of one's own body is a kind of behavior that needs to be analyzed, but as the source of data for a science it is largely of historical interest only.

◆ CHAPTER 2 ◆

The Origins of Cognitive Thought

W**hat is felt when one has a feeling is a condition of one's body, and the word used to describe it almost always comes from the word for the cause of the condition felt. The evidence is to be found in the history of the language—in the etymology of the words that refer to feelings (see Chapter 1). Etymology is the archaeology of thought. The great authority in English is the *Oxford English Dictionary* (1928), but a smaller work such as Skeat's *Etymological Dictionary of the English Language* (1956) will usually suffice. We do not have all the facts we should like to have, because the earliest meanings of many words have been lost, but we have enough to make a plausible general case. To describe great pain, for example, we say *agony*. The word first meant struggling or wrestling, a familiar cause of great pain. When other things felt the same way, the same word was used.

A similar case is made here for the words we use to refer to states of mind or cognitive processes. They almost always began as references either to some aspect of behavior or to the setting in which behavior occurred. Only very slowly have they become the vocabulary of something called mind. *Experience* is a good example. As Raymond Williams (1976) has pointed out, the word was not used to refer to anything felt or introspectively observed until the 19th century. Before that time it meant, quite literally, something a person had "gone through" (from the Latin *expiriri*), or what we should now call an exposure to contingencies of reinforcement. This paper reviews about 80 other words for states of mind or cognitive processes. They are grouped according to the bodily conditions that prevail when we are doing things, sensing things, changing the way we do or sense things (learning), staying changed (remembering), wanting, waiting, thinking, and "using our minds."

13

DOING

The word *behave* is a latecomer. The older word was *do*. As the very long entry in the *Oxford English Dictionary* (1928) shows, *do* has always emphasized consequences—the effect one has on the world. We describe much of what we ourselves do with the words we use to describe what others do. When asked, "What *did* you do?", "What *are* you doing?", or "What *are you going to do*?" we say, for example, "I wrote a letter," "I am reading a good book," or "I shall watch television." But how can we describe what we feel or introspectively observe at the time?

There is often very little to observe. Behavior often seems spontaneous; it simply happens. We say it "occurs" as in "It occurred to me to go for a walk." We often replace "it" with "thought" or "idea" ("The thought—or idea—occurred to me to go for a walk"), but what, if anything, occurs is the walk. We also say that behavior comes into our possession. We announce the happy appearance of the solution to a problem by saying "I have it!"

We report an early stage of behaving when we say, "I *feel* like going for a walk." That may mean "I feel as I have felt in the past when I have set out for a walk." What is felt may also include something of the present occasion, as if to say, "Under these conditions I often go for a walk" or it may include some state of deprivation or aversive stimulation, as if to say, "I need a breath of fresh air."

The bodily condition associated with a high probability that we shall behave or do something is harder to pin down and we resort to metaphor. Since things often fall in the direction in which they lean, we say we are *inclined* to do something, or have an *inclination* to do it. If we are strongly inclined, we may even say we are *bent* on doing it. Since things also often move in the direction in which they are pulled, we say that we *tend* to do things (from the Latin *tendere*, to stretch or extend) or that our behavior expresses an *intention*, a cognitive process widely favored by philosophers at the present time.

We also use *attitude* to refer to probability. An attitude is the *position*, *posture*, or *pose* we take when we are about to do something. For example, the pose of actors suggests something of what they are engaged in doing or are likely to do in a moment. The same sense of pose is found in *dispose* and *propose* ("I am *disposed* to go for a walk," "I *propose* to go for a walk"). Originally a synonym of *propose*, *purpose* has caused a great deal of trouble. Like other words suggesting probable action, it seems to point to the future. The future cannot be acting now, however, and elsewhere in science purpose has given way to words referring to *past* consequences. When philosophers speak of intention, for example, they are almost always speaking of operant behavior.

As an experimental analysis has shown, behavior is shaped and maintained by its consequences, but only by consequences that lie in the past. We do what we do because of what *has* happened, not what *will* happen. Unfortunately, what has happened leaves few observable traces, and why we do what we do and how likely we are to do it are therefore largely beyond the reach of introspection. Perhaps that is why, as we shall see later, behavior has so often been attributed to an initiating, originating, or creative act of will.

SENSING

To respond effectively to the world around us, we must see, hear, smell, taste, or feel it. The ways in which behavior is brought under the control of stimuli can be analyzed without too much trouble, but what we observe when we see ourselves seeing something is the source of a great misunderstanding. We say we *perceive* the world in the literal sense of taking it in (from the Latin *per* and *capere*, to take). (*Comprehend* is a close synonym, part of which comes from *prehendere*, to seize or grasp.) We say, "I take your meaning." Since we cannot take in the world itself, it has been assumed that we must make a copy. Making a copy cannot be all there is to seeing, however, because we still have to see the copy. Copy theory involves an infinite regress. Some cognitive psychologists have tried to avoid it by saying that what is taken in is a representation— perhaps a digital rather than an analog copy. When we recall ("call up an image of") what we have seen, however, we see something that looks pretty much like what we saw in the first place, and that would be an analog copy. Another way to avoid the regress is to say that at some point we *interpret* the copy or representation. The origins of *interpret* are obscure, but the word seems to have had some connection with price; an interpreter was once a broker. *Interpret* seems to have meant evaluate. It can best be understood as something we do.

The metaphor of copy theory has obvious sources. When things reinforce our looking at them, we continue to look. We keep a few such things near us so that we can look at them whenever we like. If we cannot keep the things themselves, we make copies of them, such as paintings or photographs. *Image*, a word for an internal copy, comes from the Latin *imago*. It first meant a colored bust, rather like a wax-work museum effigy. Later it meant ghost. *Effigy*, by the way, is well chosen as a word for a copy, because it first meant something constructed—from the Latin *fingere*. There is no evidence, however, that we construct anything when we see the world around us or when we see that we are seeing it.

A behavioral account of sensing is simpler. Seeing is behaving and, like all behaving, is to be explained either by natural selection (many animals respond visually shortly after birth) or operant conditioning. We do not see the world by taking it in and processing it. The world takes control of behavior when either survival or reinforcement has been contingent upon it. That can occur only when something is done about what is seen. Seeing is only part of behaving; it is behaving up to the point of action. Since behavior analysts deal only with complete instances of behavior, the sensing part is out of reach of their instruments and methods and must, as we shall see later, be left to physiologists.

CHANGING AND STAYING CHANGED

Learning is not doing; it is changing what we do. We may see that behavior has changed, but we do not see the changing. We see reinforcing consequences but not *how* they cause a change. Since the observable effects of reinforcement are usually not immediate, we often overlook the connection. Behavior is then often said to grow or *develop. Develop* originally meant to unfold, as one unfolds a letter. We assume that what we see was there from the start. Like pre-Darwinian evolution (where to evolve meant to unroll as one unrolled a scroll), developmentalism is a form of creationism.

Copies or representations play an important part in cognitive theories of learning and memory, where they raise problems that do not arise in a behavioral analysis. When we must describe something that is no longer present, the traditional view is that we recall the copy we have stored. In a behavioral analysis, contingencies of reinforcement change the way we respond to stimuli. It is a changed person, not a memory, that has been "stored."

Storage and retrieval become much more complicated when we learn and recall how something is done. It is easy to make copies of things we see, but how can we make copies of the things we do? We can model behavior for someone to imitate, but a model cannot be stored. The traditional solution is to go digital. We say the organism learns and stores rules. When, for example, a hungry rat presses a lever and receives food and the rate of pressing immediately increases, cognitive psychologists want to say that the rat has learned a rule. It now knows and can remember that "pressing the lever produces food." But "pressing the lever produces food" is our description of the contingencies we have built into the apparatus. We have no reason to suppose that the rat formulates and stores such a description. The contingencies change the rat, which then survives as a changed rat. As members of a verbal species we can

The Origins of Cognitive Thought

describe contingencies of reinforcement, and we often do because the descriptions have many practical uses (for example, we can memorize them and say them again whenever circumstances demand it) but there is no introspective or other evidence that we verbally describe every contingency that affects our behavior, and much evidence to the contrary.

Some of the words we use to describe subsequent occurrences of behavior suggest storage. *Recall*—call back—is obviously one of them; *recollect* suggests "bringing together" stored pieces. Under the influence of the computer, cognitive psychologists have turned to *retrieve*—literally "to find again" (cf. the French *trouver*), presumably after a search. The etymology of *remember,* however, does not imply storage. From the Latin *memor,* it means to be "mindful of again" and that usually means to do again what we did before. To remember what something looks like is to do what we did when we saw it. We needed no copy then, and we need none now. (We *recognize* things in the sense of "re-cognizing" them—responding to them now as we did in the past.) As a thing, a memory must be something stored, but as an action "memorizing" simply means doing what we must do to ensure that we can behave again as we are behaving now.

WANTING

Many cognitive terms describe bodily states that arise when strong behavior cannot be executed because a necessary condition is lacking. The source of a general word for states of that kind is obvious: when something is wanting, we say we *want* it. In dictionary terms, to *want* is to "suffer from the want of." *Suffer* originally meant "to undergo," but now it means "to be in pain," and strong wanting can indeed be painful. We escape from it by doing anything that has been reinforced by the thing that is now wanting and wanted.

A near synonym of *want* is *need*. It, too, was first tied closely to suffering; to be in need was to be under restraint or duress. (Words tend to come into use when the conditions they describe are conspicuous.) *Felt* is often added: one has a *felt need*. We sometimes distinguish between want and need on the basis of the immediacy of the consequence. Thus, we *want* something to eat, but we *need* a taxi in order to do something that will have later consequences.

Wishing and *hoping* are also states of being unable to do something we are strongly inclined to do. The putted golf ball rolls across the green, but we can only *wish* or *will* it into the hole. (*Wish* is close to *will*. The Anglo-Saxon *willan* meant "wish," and the *would* in "Would that it were so" is not close to the past tense of will.)

Theoretical Issues

When something we need is missing, we say we *miss* it. When we want something for a long time, we say we *long* for it. We long to see someone we love who has long been absent.

When past consequences have been aversive, we do not hope, wish, or long for them. Instead, we *worry* or feel *anxious* about them. *Worry* first meant "choke" (a dog worries the rat it has caught), and *anxious* comes from another word for choke. We cannot do anything about things that have already happened, though we are still affected by them. We say we are *sorry* for a mistake we have made. *Sorry* is a weak form of *sore*. As the slang expression has it, we may be "sore about something." We *resent* mistreatment, quite literally, by "feeling it again" (*resent* and *sentiment* share a root).

Sometimes we cannot act appropriately because we do not have the appropriate behavior. When we have lost our way, for example, we say we feel *lost*. To be *bewildered* is like being in a wilderness. In such a case, we *wander* ("wend our way aimlessly") or *wonder* what to do. The wonders of the world were so unusual that no one responded to them in normal ways. We stand in *awe* of such things, and *awe* comes from a Greek word that meant "anguish" or "terror." *Anguish*, like *anxiety*, once meant "choked," and *terror* was a violent trembling. A *miracle*, from the Latin *admirare*, is "something to be wondered at," or about.

Sometimes we cannot respond because we are taken unawares; we are *surprised* (the second syllable of which comes from the Latin *prehendere*, "to seize or grasp"). The story of Dr. Johnson's wife is a useful example. Finding the doctor kissing the maid, she is said to have exclaimed, "I am surprised!" "No," said the doctor, "*I* am surprised; *you* are astonished!" *Astonished*, like *astounded*, first meant "to be alarmed by thunder." Compare the French *étonner* and *tonnere*.

When we cannot easily do something because our behavior has been mildly punished, we are *embarrassed* or barred. Conflicting responses find us *perplexed:* they are "interwoven" or "entangled." When a response has been inconsistently reinforced, we are *diffident*, in the sense of not trusting. *Trust* comes from a Teutonic root suggesting consolation, which in turn has a distant Greek relative meaning "whole." Trust is bred by consistency.

WAITING

Wanting, wishing, worrying, resenting, and the like are often called "feelings." More likely to be called "states of mind" are the bodily conditions that result from certain special temporal arrangements of stimuli, responses, and reinforcers. The temporal arrangements are much easier to analyze than the states of mind that are said to result.

Watch is an example. It first meant "to be awake." The night watch was someone who stayed awake. The word *alert* comes from the Italian for "a military watch." We watch television until we fall asleep.

Those who are awake may be *aware* of what they are doing; aware is close to *wary* or *cautious*. (*Cautious* comes from a word familiar to us in *caveat emptor.*) Psychologists have been especially interested in awareness, although they have generally used a synonym, *consciousness.*

One who watches may be waiting for something to happen, but *waiting* is more than watching. It is something we all do but may not think of as a state of mind. Consider waiting for a bus. Nothing we have ever done has made the bus arrive, but its arrival has reinforced many of the things we do while waiting. For example, we stand where we have most often stood and look in the direction in which we have most often looked when buses have appeared. Seeing a bus has also been strongly reinforced, and we may see one while we are waiting, either in the sense of "thinking what one would look like" or by mistaking a truck for a bus.

Waiting for something to happen is also called *expecting,* a more prestigious cognitive term. To *expect* is "to look forward to" (from the Latin *expectare*). To *anticipate* is "to do other things beforehand," such as getting the bus fare ready. Part of the word comes from the Latin *capere*— "to take." Both expecting and anticipating are forms of behavior that have been adventitiously reinforced by the appearance of something. (Much of what we do when we are waiting is public. Others can see us standing at a bus stop and looking in the direction from which buses come. An observant person may even see us take a step forward when a truck comes into view, or reach for a coin as the bus appears. We ourselves "see" something more, of course. The contingencies have worked private changes in us, to some of which we alone can respond.)

THINKING

It is widely believed that behavior analysts cannot deal with the cognitive processes called thinking. We often use *think* to refer to weak behavior. If we are not quite ready to say, "He is wrong," we say, "I think he is wrong." *Think* is often a weaker word for *know*; we say, "I think this is the way to do it" when we are not quite ready to say, "I know this is the way" or "This *is* the way." We also say *think* when stronger behavior is not feasible. Thus, we think of what something looks like when it is not there to see, and we think of doing something that we cannot at the moment do.

Many thought processes, however, have nothing to do with the distinction between weak and strong behavior or between private and public, overt and covert. To think is to do something that makes other behavior possible. Solving a problem is an example. A problem is a situation that does not evoke an effective response; we solve it by changing the situation until a response occurs. Telephoning a friend is a problem if we do not know the number, and we solve it by looking up the number. Etymologically, to *solve* is "to loosen or set free," as sugar is *dissolved* in coffee. This is the sense in which thinking is responsible for doing. "It is how people think that determines how they act." Hence, the hegemony of mind. But again the terms we use began as references to behavior. Here are a few examples:

1. When no effective stimulus is available we sometimes *expose* one. We *discover* things by *uncovering* them. To *detect* a signal does not mean to respond to it; it means to remove something (the *tegmen*) that covers it.

2. When we cannot uncover a stimulus, we sometimes keep an accessible one in view until a response occurs. *Observe* and *regard* both come from words that meant "to hold or keep in view," the latter from the French *garder. Consider* once meant "to look steadily at the stars until something could be made of them" (*consider* and *sidereal* have a common root). *Contemplate*, another word for *think*, once meant "to look at a template or plan of the stars." (In those days all one could do to make sense of the stars was to look at them.)

3. We not only look at things to see them better, we *look for* them. We *search* or *explore*. To look for a pen is to do what one has done in the past when a pen came into view. (A pigeon that pecks a spot because doing so has been occasionally reinforced will "look for it" after it has been taken away by doing precisely what it did when the spot was there—moving its head in ways that brought the spot into view.) We search in order to find, and we do not avoid searching by *contriving* something to be seen, because *contrive*, like *retrieve*, is from the French *trouver*, "to find."

4. We bring different things together to make a single response feasible when we *concentrate*, from an older word *concentre*, "to join in a center."

5. We do the reverse when we separate things so that we can more easily deal with them in different ways. We *sift* them, as if we

were putting them through a sieve. The *cern* in *discern* (Latin *cernere*) means "to separate or set apart."

6. We *mark* things so that we shall be more likely to notice them again. *Distinguish*, a good cognitive term, once meant "to mark by pricking." *Mark* is strongly associated with boundaries; animals mark the edges of their territories.

7. To *define* is literally "to mark the bounds or end" (*finis*) of something. We also *determine* what a word means by indicating where the referent terminates.

8. We *compare* things, literally, by "putting them side by side" so that we can more easily see whether they match. The *par* in *compare* means "equal." Par value is equal value. In golf, par is the score to be matched.

9. We *speculate* about things in the sense of looking at them from different angles, as in a *specula* or mirror.

10. *Cogitate*, an old word for *think*, first meant "to shake up." A *conjecture* is something "thrown out" for consideration. We *accept* or *reject* things that occur to us in the sense of taking or throwing them back, as if we were fishing.

11. Sometimes it helps to change one mode of stimulation into another. We do so when we convert the "heft" of an object into its weight, read on a scale. By weighing things we react more precisely to their weight. *Ponder, deliberate,* and *examine,* good cognitive processes, all once meant "to weigh." *Ponder* is part of *ponderous*, the *liber* in *deliberate* is the Latin *libra*, "a scales," and *examine* meant "the tongue of a balance."

12. We react more precisely to the number of things in a group by *counting*. One way to count is to recite *one, two, three,* and so on, while ticking off (touching) each item. Before people learned to count, they recorded the number of things in a group by letting a pebble stand for each thing. The pebbles were called *calculi* and their use *calculation*. There is a long, but unbroken, road from pebbles to silicon chips.

13. After we have thought for some time, we may reach a decision. To *decide* once meant simply to cut off or bring to an end.

14. A better word for *decide* is *conclude*, "to close a discussion." What we *conclude* about something is our last word.

It is certainly no accident that so many of the terms we now use to refer to cognitive processes once referred either to behavior or to the occasions on which behavior occurs. It could be objected, of course, that what a word once meant is not what it means now. Surely there is a difference between weighing a sack of potatoes and weighing the evidence in a court of law. When we speak of weighing evidence we are using a metaphor. But a metaphor is a word that is "carried over" from one referent to another on the basis of a common property. The common property in weighing is the conversion of one kind of thing (potatoes or evidence) into another (a number on a scale or a verdict). Once we have seen this weighing done with potatoes it is easier to see it done with evidence. Over the centuries human behavior has grown steadily more complex as it has come under the control of more complex environments. The number and complexity of the bodily conditions felt or introspectively observed have grown accordingly, and with them has grown the vocabulary of cognitive thinking.

We could also say that *weight* becomes abstract when we move from potatoes to evidence. The word is indeed abstracted in the sense of its being drawn away from its original referent, but it continues to refer to a common property, and, as in the case of metaphor, in a possibly more decisive way. The testimony in a trial is much more complex than a sack of potatoes, and "guilty" probably implies more than "ten pounds." But abstraction is not a matter of complexity. Quite the contrary. Weight is only one aspect of a potato, and guilt is only one aspect of a person. Weight is as abstract as guilt. It is only under verbal contingencies of reinforcement that we respond to single properties of things or persons. In doing so we abstract the property from the thing or person.

One may still argue that at some point the term is abstracted and carried over, not to a slightly more complex case, but to something of a very different kind. Potatoes are weighed in the physical world; evidence is weighed in the *mind*, or with *the help* of the mind, or *by* the mind. And that brings us to the heart of the matter.

MIND

The battle cry of the cognitive revolution is "Mind is back!" A "great new science of mind" is born. Behaviorism nearly destroyed our concern for it, but behaviorism has been overthrown, and we can take up again where the philosophers and early psychologists left off.

Extraordinary things have certainly been said about the mind. The finest achievements of the species have been attributed to it; it is said to work at miraculous speeds in miraculous ways. But what it is and what it does are still far from clear. We all speak of the mind with little or no hesitation, but we pause when asked for a definition. Dictionaries are of no help. To understand what *mind* means we must first look up *perception, idea, feeling, intention,* and many other words we have just examined, and we shall find each of them defined with the help of the others. Perhaps it is of the very essence of mind that it cannot be defined. Nevertheless, we can see how the word is used and what people seem to be saying when they use it.

Mind is often spoken of as if it were a place. When it occurs to us to do something, we say that "it comes to mind." If we go on doing it, it is because we "keep it in mind." We miss an appointment when it "slips our mind." Mind is also spoken of as an organ. People "use their minds" to solve problems. It may be significant that we are more likely to say, "Use your *head*" or "Use your *brains*" than "Use your mind," as if we felt the need for something more substantial. *Mind* also sometimes means "made more likely to act." An early use ("I was minded to go") still survives in *remind*. An appointment book reminds us of an appointment, and someone we meet reminds us of a friend if we respond to some extent as we respond to the friend.

Often, however, *mind* means little more than "do." "I have a mind to tell you" means "I am inclined to tell you." Those who "speak their mind" say what they have to say. We are cautioned to avoid falling by "minding the step" in the sense of noticing it. Students "mind their teachers" in the sense of obeying them, and teachers "mind their students" in the sense of watching them. "Do you mind my smoking?" means "Do you object?" In reply to "will you have a drink?", "I don't mind if I do" means "I won't refuse if you offer me one."

The mind that the cognitive revolution has restored to prominence is also the doer of things. It is the executor of cognitive processes. It perceives the world, organizes sense data into meaningful wholes, and processes information. It is the double of the person whose mind it is, a replica, a surrogate, a Doppelgänger. Take any sentence in which the mind does something and see if the meaning is substantially changed if you substitute person. It is said, for example, that "the mind cannot comprehend infinity." Does that mean anything more than that no person can comprehend infinity? Cognitive processes are behavioral processes; they are things people do.

That they are something more, that what we feel as we behave is the cause of our behaving, is the crucial age-old mistake. From the time of the early Greeks, the search has been on for internal determiners. The heart, lungs, liver, kidneys, spleen, not to mention the humors, and at last the brain have all been promising candidates. As organs, they have had the advantage that they could be observed in a possibly more reliable way in dead bodies, but philosophers were soon contending that perceptions, feelings, intentions, and the like had an independent existence. Unfortunately, we cannot report any internal event, physical or metaphysical, accurately. The words we use are words we learned from people who did not know precisely what we were talking about, and we have no sensory nerves going to the parts of the brain in which the most important events presumably occur. Many cognitive psychologists recognize these limitations and dismiss the words we have been examining as the language of "common sense psychology." The mind that has made its comeback is therefore not the mind of Locke or Berkeley or of Wundt or William James. We do not observe it; we infer it. We do not see ourselves processing information, for example. We see the materials that we process and the product, but not the producing. We now treat mental processes like intelligence, personality, or character traits—as things no one ever claims to see through introspection. Whether or not the cognitive revolution has restored mind as the proper subject matter of psychology, it has not restored introspection as the proper way of looking at it. The behaviorists' attack on introspection has been devastating.

Cognitive psychologists have therefore turned to brain science and computer science to confirm their theories. Brain science, they say, will eventually tell us what cognitive processes really are. They will answer, once and for all, the old questions about monism, dualism, and interactionism. By building machines that do what people do, computer science will demonstrate how the mind works.

What is wrong with all this is not what philosophers, psychologists, brain scientists, and computer scientists have found or will find; the error is the direction in which they are looking. No account of what is happening inside the human body, no matter how complete, will explain the origins of human behavior. What happens inside the body is not a beginning. By looking at how a clock is built, we can explain why it keeps good time, but not why keeping time is important, or how the clock came to be built that way. We must ask the same questions about a person. Why do people do what they do, and why do the bodies that do it have the structures they have? We can trace a small part of human behavior, and a much larger part of the behavior of other species, to natural selection and the evolution of the species, but the greater part of human behavior must be traced to contingencies of reinforcement, especially to the very complex social contingencies we call cultures. Only when we take those histories into account can we explain why people behave as they do.

That position is sometimes characterized as treating a person as a black box and ignoring its contents. Behavior analysts would study the invention and uses of clocks without asking how clocks are built. But nothing is being ignored. Behavior analysts leave what is inside the black box to those who have the instruments and methods needed to study it properly. There are two unavoidable gaps in any behavioral account: one between the stimulating action of the environment and the response of the organism, and one between consequences and the resulting change in behavior. Only brain science can fill those gaps. In doing so it completes the account; it does not give a different account of the same thing. Human behavior will eventually be explained, because it can only be explained by the cooperative action of ethology, brain science, and behavior analysis.

The analysis of behavior need not wait until brain science has done its part. The behavioral facts will not be changed, and they suffice for both a science and a technology. Brain science may discover other kinds of variables affecting behavior, but it will turn to a behavioral analysis for the clearest account of their effects.

CONCLUSION

Verbal contingencies of reinforcement explain why we report what we feel or introspectively observe. The verbal culture that arranges such contingencies would not have evolved if it had not been useful. Bodily conditions are not the causes of behavior but they are collateral effects of the causes, and people's answers to questions about how they feel or what they are thinking often tell us something about what has happened to them or what they have done. We can understand them better and are more likely to anticipate what they will do. The words they use are part of a living language that can be used without embarrassment by cognitive psychologists and behavior analysts alike in their daily lives.

But not in their science! A few traditional terms may survive in the technical language of a science, but they are carefully defined and stripped by usage of their old connotations. Science requires a language. We seem to be giving up the effort to explain our behavior by reporting what we feel or introspectively observe in our bodies, but we have only begun to construct a science needed to analyze the complex interactions between the environment and the body and the behavior to which it gives rise.

◆ CHAPTER 3 ◆

The Initiating Self

Is there a place in a scientific analysis of behavior for an initiating, originating, creative self? Having dispensed with God as a creator, must science also dispense with that image of God called Man? We feel the need for a creative god because we see the world but very little of the processes through which it came into existence, the product but not the production. Perhaps it is because we see human behavior but very little of the process through which it comes into existence that we feel the need for a creative self. With behavior, however, we have other evidence: We can see or introspectively observe our own bodies as we behave, and it is possible that what we see is the process of creation. Call it mind or will. Is it only retrospectively that we have attributed the creation of the world to a greater Mind or Will—to a god in the image of Man?

It does not matter, because science has changed all that. Astronomers may have no explanation of the big bang, but they are giving an increasingly plausible account of the formation of the chemical elements and of their distribution in space. Chemistry suggests ways in which living things could have emerged from nonliving, and biologists explain the origin of species, including *homo sapiens*, through natural selection. There is less for a creator to do.

Behavior has also come within the scope of a scientific analysis. It is the product of three kinds of selection, the first of which, natural selection, is the field of ethology. The second, operant conditioning, is the field of behavior analysis. The third, the evolution of the social contingencies of reinforcement we call cultures, explains the large repertoires of behavior characteristic of the human species.

The terms we use to designate a behaving individual depend upon the type of selection. Natural selection gives us *organism,* operant conditioning gives us *person,* and, it will be argued here, the evolution of cultures gives us *self.* An organism is more than a body; it is a body that does things. Both *organ* and *organism* are etymologically related to *work.* The organism is the executor. *Person* is derived from the word for the masks through which actors spoke their lines in Greek and Roman theater. A mask identified the role the actor was playing; it marked him as a character. By wearing different masks, he could play different roles. Contingencies of operant reinforcement have rather similar effects. Starting with the organism that has evolved through natural selection, they build the behavioral repertoires called persons. Different contingencies build different persons, possibly within the same skin, as the classical examples of multiple personalities show.

In a long chapter called "Self-control" in *Science and Human Behavior* (1953), I used *self* very much as I would now use *person.* I reviewed techniques through which a person manipulated the environmental variables of which his behavior was a function and distinguished between controlling and controlled selves, defining them as repertoires of behavior. But that was thirty years ago, and behavioristic theory has advanced. A clearer distinction can now be made between person and self: a person, as a repertoire of behavior, can be observed by others; the self, as a set of accompanying internal states, is observed only through feeling or introspection.

Several problems of usage must be mentioned. We need the word *self* as a reflexive pronoun because there are other people in the world. The self I see in a mirror or video recording is the person others see. "I made it myself" means little more than that I was the one who made it. Webster's *Third New International Dictionary* (1981) contains about 500 entries beginning with *self,* and in some of them the word is merely reflexive.

That is not the self we are considering here, however. Only under special kinds of verbal contingencies do we respond to certain features of our body. Looking back at an unusual occasion, I may report that "I was a different person," but others could say the same thing. "I was not myself," however, suggests that I *felt* like a different person. The self is what a person *feels like.* It is the self we know when we follow the advice of the Delphic oracle, "Know thyself," and it is the self we change when, in response to the injunction "Behave yourself," we do more than "behave differently."

There is another problem of usage. The English language evolved when it was generally believed that behavior started within the individual.

The Initiating Self

One sensed the environment and acted upon it. In a behavioral analysis the environment acts first, in either of two ways. As a consequence it reinforces behavior and an operant comes into existence. As a setting it elicits or evokes behavior. Few English words, certainly not *person* or *self*, are at home in such a behavioral version. We are more readily understood when we ask why people observe certain conditions of their bodies than when we ask why the conditions evoke self-observation. The traditional version can scarcely be avoided in practical use, or in paraphrasing technical expressions, even though the self then remains the very initiator whose existence we are questioning.

In what follows, however, we shall look at a different interpretation of several common examples.

SELF-OBSERVATION

Under what verbal contingencies of reinforcement, for example, do we observe our self and report that we are doing so? An organism seldom behaves effectively without responding to its own body. The contingencies responsible for the behavior explain that kind of self-stimulation. Very different contingencies account for self-observation. The first to evolve may have been associated with modeling. To model is to behave in ways that are easily observed and imitated, first by others but possibly also by the modelers themselves. Operant modeling, and the self-observation it facilitates, appears to be exclusively human; reinforcement from the behavior of an imitator is apparently too long delayed to reinforce modeling in other species. (Deferred consequences raise no problem for the modeling due to natural selection, because the survival of the species is necessarily a deferred consequence.)

Contingencies promoting self-observation must have multiplied rapidly with the advent of vocal verbal behavior. (Modeling is verbal, although not necessarily vocal, in the sense that the reinforcement is mediated by other persons: we cannot imitate unless there is a model, and we are not modeling unless our behavior has been imitated.) When the vocal musculature of the human species came under operant control, people could tell others what to do as well as show them, and it must then have been much easier to see and to talk about what they themselves were doing. (Doing includes sensing, of course. We not only observe that we do things, we observe that we see things.)

Many verbal contingencies promoting self-observation are more explicit. People are asked to report what they are doing or why they are doing it, and when they reply they may tell themselves as well as others. Psychotherapy is often an effort to improve self-observation, to bring more of what is done and why it is done "into consciousness." In both psychotherapy and literature, character analysis is often called a "search for the self." More often, it is a search for the "real self," a self that must be searched for presumably because it has been hidden. Behavior is most often hidden, from oneself as well as from others, when it has been punished, and that may explain why the real self is so often badly behaved. Witness the self that is said to have been exposed by de Sade. (In such a case "real" could mean "primitive," because what is felt is due either to natural selection or to reinforcing consequences—food, sex, and aggressive damage—similar to consequences that must have played a predominant role in natural selection.)

SELF-ESTEEM

A culture commends and rewards those of its members who do useful or interesting things, in part by calling them and the things they do good or right. In the process, behavior is positively reinforced, and bodily conditions are generated that may be observed and valued by the person whose self it is. It is a self that is especially vulnerable to scientific analysis. I have pointed to a parallel in natural selection. For example, a woman has a baby. It is her baby and we give her credit for her achievement. Geneticists, however, tell us that she is not responsible for any of its features. She gave it half its genes, but she got them from her own father and mother. She has sheltered and nourished the growing fetus, but she has made no other contribution. In saying so, however, we seem to rob her of the credit she has received for having the baby and hence destroy her sense of worth.

An operant parallel is not as simple. A poet "has" a poem in the sense of having written it. It is his poem. Critics will show "influences," however, and if we knew enough about what the poet had read and done, we could presumably explain the whole poem. That seems to invalidate any commendation the poet has received from others and destroys his own sense of worth.

THE RESPONSIBLE SELF

The self that one esteems appears to be a product of the positively reinforcing practices of a social environment, but cultures more often control their members with aversive stimuli, either as negative reinforcers that strengthen wanted behavior or as punishments that suppress unwanted behavior. Cultures thus hold their members *responsible* for what they have done, and members "feel responsible."

They seldom protest, however, when a behavioral analysis shifts the responsibility from them to the environment. (The juvenile delinquent readily agrees that his early environment is responsible for his delinquency.) Instead, the usual response to a behavioral analysis is to protest the control it demonstrates, whether positive or negative. Thus, withholding food from a prisoner so that it can be used as a positive reinforcer is protested as a violation of the right to freedom from want, and the use of aversive stimuli, either as negative reinforcers or as punishment, is protested as a violation of the right to freedom from fear.

SELF-CONFIDENCE

Even though we are not actually in control of our behavior, is it not important that we *believe* we are? Is it not true that only when we believe in ourselves do we do our best? But the self in which we have faith may be a product of doing well rather than the cause. When at last I have got the top off the child-proof aspirin bottle and exclaim, "I've done it!" I report an instance of behavior. If someone asks me whether I can get the top off and I say, "I believe I can," I am either making a prediction based upon past successes or reporting a bodily condition resulting from them. People who are not successful in what they do may lose faith in themselves, but a counselor may restore faith by reminding them of overlooked successes, thus restoring something of the bodily state they once felt. A more effective way of restoring belief in oneself, of course, is to restore successes, perhaps by simplifying contingencies of reinforcement.

A more immediate effect of success is often called self-confidence. The tennis player who makes a series of bad shots "loses confidence" and is often said to make other bad shots because he has lost it. A brilliant shot "restores his confidence," and he plays better. To put it another way, however, bad shots extinguish behavior in the sense of reducing its probability of occurrence, and good shots recondition it. One who has played badly may be at the point of giving up tennis altogether until a very successful day "changes his mind" in the sense of changing the probability of his playing. If the self-confidence gained from one fine play extends to a whole repertoire, better play is more likely to be due to what sportscasters called improved "concentration." The more strongly inclined one is to play, the less likely one is to be distracted.

THE RATIONAL SELF

A different self seems to be felt when engaging in rule-governed behavior. That must have been the case when *person* meant the mask through which an actor spoke, because actors do not speak their own lines. They say and do what they are told to say and do. That is also true of those who take advice, observe rules, and obey laws. If that is all they do, they are not "being themselves." The bodily conditions they feel are not the products of contingencies to which they themselves have been exposed; they are indirect products of the contingencies which have affected those who gave the advice or formulated the rules. Only when advice has been taken, rules observed or laws obeyed, and reinforcing consequences have followed can "the real self" be felt.

Actors "know what they are saying," however, in the sense that they know their lines before they say them, and something of the sort may be said of those who take advice, observe rules, and obey laws. They "know what they are doing" in the sense that it has already been put into words. People who formulate descriptions of contingencies for their own use "know what they are doing" in that way and are said to act rationally. In reply to the question "Why did you do that?" one may simply mention a felt or introspectively observed state ("I wanted to do it" or "I felt like doing it") or one may "give a reason" by alluding to a controlling variable ("I intended to get a drink" or "I was afraid the rope would break"). Reasons are not consequences, however; they are names of consequences.

We are said to have acted rationally when we can give reasons for our behavior, but most of our behavior is not rational in that sense. Contingencies of selection affect our behavior whether or not we recognize them. Freud is perhaps responsible for the fact that "rationalizing" suggests giving the *wrong* reasons. These are issues, however, which more directly concern the mind rather than the self.

THE MIND AND THE SELF

As the word for a felt or introspectively observed state that accompanies behavior, *self* is obviously close to *mind*. Whenever the mind is said to do something, it is usually possible to substitute *organism* or *person*. The "vast resources of the human mind," for example, are the vast resources of the human species. Something of the sort can also be said of the self, but a useful distinction can still be made. Like the distinction between thinking and doing, it concerns the order of events. "I changed my mind" is not far from "I changed what I was *on the point of* doing." Mind seems to be something "farther back inside" than self and is therefore even more likely to be mistaken for an originator. A further step back would, of course, reach the environmental contingencies.

SUMMARY

We have looked at several selves of which people often speak. They include (a) a self observed (a bodily condition that accompanies behavior), (b) a self esteemed (a bodily condition resulting from commendation by others or self-commendation learned from others), (c) a confident self (the accompaniment of positively reinforced behavior), (d) a responsible self (an accompaniment of the product of aversive contingencies), and (e) a rational self (an accompaniment of behavior governed by rules, including rules made by the behaving person). We have traced them to contingencies of reinforcement responsible for both the behavior and the bodily conditions accompanying it, and the necessarily verbal contingencies responsible for observing, esteeming, feeling confident, responsible, and rational.

Shall we ever be able to say more about what is felt? Almost certainly not through introspection. We do not have sensory nerves going to relevant parts of the body or any chance of agreeing upon words that refer to private events of any kind. Eventually, the body will be more accurately observed in a different way by physiology, especially neurology, but it will then be observed as the product of specifiable contingencies of variation and selection rather than as what was less accurately seen through introspection.

Almost every field of science has two languages, one for the things observed casually in daily life and one presumably for the same things observed with the instruments and methods of science. The field of human behavior has had a third, referring to things within the observer felt or introspectively observed. The reflexive "self" is part of the first language, and the "selves" we have been discussing are part of the third. Both the first and the third have many practical uses, the third because when people tell us how they feel, they report the effect of what has happened to them, from which we often infer something of what happened. The *use* of the word *self* is verbal behavior, and as such is a referent of the second language, but to answer the question with which we began, the *word self* itself is not part of that language.

◆ CHAPTER 4 ◆

The Listener

In the traditional view of a speech episode, held by philosophers for thousands of years, the speaker perceives some part of the world in the literal sense of capturing or taking it in (or rather, since there is no room for the world itself, taking in a copy or representation). The speaker then puts the copy into words, the meanings of which correspond in some way with what the speaker perceived. The listener takes the meanings out of the words and composes another copy or representation. The listener thus *receives* or *conceives* what the speaker has *perceived*. Something has been communicated in the sense of being made common to both speaker and listener. A message has been sent, the content of which is sometimes called information. Information theory, however, was invented to deal only with the structural features of a message (how many bits or bytes can be sent through a telephone line or stored in a computer). The content of a message is more appropriately called *knowledge*, from a root which gave the Greek word *gnomein*, the Latin *gnoscere*, the late-Latin *co-gnitio*, and at last our own *cognition*.

In a behavioral account, the direction of action is exactly reversed. Speakers do not take in the world and put it into words; they respond to it in ways which have been shaped and maintained by special contingencies of reinforcement. Listeners do not extract information or knowledge from words and compose secondhand copies of the world; they respond to verbal stimuli in ways which have been shaped and maintained by other contingencies of reinforcement. Both contingencies are maintained by an evolved verbal environment or culture.

That is a great difference—as great, perhaps, as the difference between creation and natural selection in evolutionary theory. The origin

35

of behavior raises quite as many problems as the origin of species. A minor problem is that in using modern English, you find yourself implying the traditional view in the very act of challenging it. Only at special times can you be technical and correct. The rest of the time everyday English must suffice, and you must expect to be accused of inconsistency.

The problem is especially hard to solve when the behavior is verbal. Speakers are not initiators. Neither in the evolution of a verbal environment nor in the conditioning of speakers and listeners does speaking come first. There must be a listener before there can be a speaker. The same seems to be true of the signaling behavior of other species. Something one animal does (making a noise, moving in a given way, leaving a trace) becomes a signal only when another animal responds to it.

Most of my book *Verbal Behavior* (1957) was about the speaker. It contained a few diagrams showing interactions between speakers and listeners, but little direct discussion of listening. I could justify that because, except when the listener was also to some extent speaking, listening was not verbal in the sense of being effective only through the mediation of other persons. But if listeners are responsible for the behavior of speakers, we need to look more closely at what they do.

THE VERBAL OPERANT

When we say that behavior is controlled by the environment, we mean two very different things. The environment shapes and maintains repertoires of behavior, but it also serves as the occasion upon which behavior occurs. The concept of the operant makes this distinction. We say that we reinforce a response when we make a reinforcer contingent upon it, but we do not change that particular response. What we reinforce, in the sense of strengthen, is the operant, the probability that similar responses will occur in the future. That is more than the distinction between class and member of a class. My paper *The Generic Nature of the Concepts of Stimulus and Response* (1935) was about classes. Responses are never exactly alike, but orderly changes appear if we count only those instances which have a defining property. An operant is a class of responses, not an instance, but it is also a probability.

When that distinction is ignored, references to behavior are often ambiguous. Nest building, for example, can mean (a) a *kind* of behavior (something birds characteristically do), (b) a *probability* of behaving ("Nest building appears shortly after mating"), and (c) an *instance* ("The bird is building a nest"). Similarly, pressing a lever can mean (a) a *kind* of behavior (something operant conditioners often study), (b) a *probability* (pressing is strengthened when a response is followed by a reinforcer), and (c) an *instance* ("The rat is pressing the lever"). Something of the sort may be said of cultural practices. Plowing is (a) a *kind* of behavior ("Plowing first appeared in ancient Mesopotamia and Egypt"), (b) a *probability* (plowing depends upon the weather), and (c) an *instance* ("The farmer is plowing his field").

Similar distinctions are crucial in speaking of verbal behavior:

1. A *language* is a *kind* of behavior (English, Arabic, and so on). It exists even though no one is speaking it. (No one need speak it at all if it is a dead language.) Its practices are recorded in dictionaries (which give meanings only as words having the same meanings) and in grammars (rules describing conventional arrangements of words).
2. A *verbal operant* is a *probability.* Five kinds of operants—mand, tact, intraverbal, echoic, and textual—are distinguished by their respective contingencies of reinforcement. They are maintained by verbal environments or cultures—that is, by listeners.
3. The verbal behavior we observe and study is composed of *instances,* with respect to which listeners play their second role as part of the occasion on which behavior occurs. We call a verbal response a mand or a tact, but only to indicate the kind of reinforcing history responsible for its occurrence. It would be more precise, but less convenient, to say mand-response or tact-response, using *mand* and *tact* as nouns to refer to operants and as adjectives to identify kinds of instances. *Intraverbal, echoic,* and *textual* are already adjectives, and we convert them into nouns to refer to operants. (Incidentally, the difference between an operant and a response is not the difference between competence and performance. A performance is a response, but a probability of responding is more than merely being *able* to respond. The difference between probability and instance is also not the difference between a verbal operant and an assertion.)

There is no very good word for the occurrence of a verbal response. *Utter* simply means to "outer" or "bring behavior out," not to have any effect on a listener. *Speak* first meant merely to make a noise (a gun can speak). *Say* and *tell,* however, imply effects on listeners. We say or tell something to someone. When we ask what someone has said, we may be given either the same words (the utterance) or other words having the same effect on the listener and hence "saying the same thing." Let us look at some of the major effects on the listener which shape and maintain the behavior of the speaker.

The Listener Is Told

In one type of speech episode, speaker and listener compose what would otherwise be one person. If there is no doorman at a hotel, we go to the curb and hail a taxi. To a doorman, however, we say, "Taxi, please." *Taxi* is a mand, and the doorman hails a taxi. (The *please* is an autoclitic. It identifies *taxi*, not only as a mand, but as the particular kind called a request.) If, on the other hand, we have ordered a taxi and are waiting for it in the lobby, and the doorman comes and says *taxi* when it arrives, that is a tact, and we respond as if we had seen the taxi ourselves. The mand frees us from making a response. The tact replaces a discriminative stimulus controlling a response.

Verbal behavior usually occurs in larger samples called sentences. Whole sentences may be operants, but most are put together or "composed" on the spot. (Since a sentence may never have occurred before if the conditions responsible for its parts have never occurred before, the number of potential sentences is therefore infinite. They are presumably realizable only in infinite time, however.)

Traditionally, a sentence is said to "express" something, again in the sense of "bringing it out." Until it has been expressed, the something is presumably accessible only through introspection, and is usually called a thought. A sentence is also said to express a feeling. (The word *sentence* is etymologically close to *sentiment*). What is felt is often called an intention. (We use *mean* as a synonym of *intend* when we say, "I mean to go.") The wrong meaning has been drawn from what is said if the listener does not do what the speaker "intended."

Since introspective evidence of feelings and states of mind still resists systematic analysis, cognitive psychologists have turned to other evidence of what is happening when a person behaves verbally. Their basic formulation is close to that of the old stimulus-response formula. People do not respond to the world about them, they "process" it as information. What that means must be inferred from what they do, however. The data consist of input and output. What is seen is processed and stored as a representation, which can be retrieved and described on a given occasion. When the something done has been reinforced, the contingencies are "processed" and stored as rules, to be retrieved and put to use. The behavior itself can be analyzed in a much simpler way by looking directly at the contingencies of reinforcement, but that is something cognitive psychologists almost never do.

The contingencies easily account for another problem that seems to be out of reach of introspection. Listeners are said to respond to what speakers say if they "trust" or "believe" them. It is simpler to say that trust and belief are simply bodily states resulting from histories of reinforcement. We use the same words for nonverbal behavior. I "believe" a small object on my desk is my pen, in the sense that I tend to pick it up when I am about to write something. I do so because when I have picked up similar objects in the past they have proved to be pens. I "trust" my chair will hold me because it always has done so.

In the long run we believe or trust those who most often qualify what they say with appropriate autoclitics. Perhaps we are more likely to respond to a speaker who says, "The door *is* unlocked" than one who says, "*I think* the door is unlocked" or "The door *may be* unlocked," but in the long run we shall believe or trust those who have added the qualifying autoclitics to tell us something about the strength of their behavior and have therefore less often misled us.

In the simplest case, then, a speaker tells a listener what to do or what has happened because listeners have reinforced similar behavior in similar situations, and the listeners have done so because in similar situations certain reinforcing consequences have followed for them.

The Listener Is Taught

Teaching is more than telling. When the doorman said, "taxi," we "learned" that a taxi was waiting, but we were not taught. When we were first told, "That's a taxi," we learned what a taxi looked like, but again we were not taught. Teaching occurs when a response is primed, in the sense of being evoked for the first time, and then reinforced. For example, a teacher models a verbal response and reinforces our repetition of it. If we cannot repeat all of it, we may need to be prompted, but eventually the behavior occurs without help.

The same two steps can be seen when we teach ourselves. We read a passage in a book (thus priming the behavior), turn away and say as much of it as we can, and turn back to the book for prompts if needed. Success in saying the passage without help is the reinforcing consequence.

Instructional contingencies in schools and colleges are designed to prepare students for contingencies of reinforcement which they will encounter at some later time. Few, if any, natural reinforcers are therefore available, and reinforcers must be contrived. Something like a spoken "right!" or "good!" or confirmation by a teaching machine must be made contingent on the behavior. Grades are almost always deferred, and the prevailing contingencies are therefore usually aversive. When we correct someone in the course of a conversation, we are also teaching. We are priming the kind of response which will not be corrected. Unfortunately, that too is usually aversive.

The Listener Is Advised

Different effects on the listener distinguish telling and teaching from advising or warning. "Look out!" is a warning; the listener looks and avoids harm—escapes being struck by a car, perhaps. "Look!" is advice; the listener looks and sees something—an interesting person passing in a car, perhaps. Those are not contrived consequences. Advice and warning bring uncontrived consequences into play.

Not all advice has the form of a mand, of course. To a friend who has expressed an interest in seafood you may say, "The Harborside Restaurant serves excellent seafood." To someone who is merely learning about the city as a place to live, that is only telling. To someone who is preparing to be a guide to the city, it is one step in teaching. Only to a listener who is looking for a particular kind of restaurant is it advice. The instructions that come with complex equipment *tell* us what the equipment will do. They *advise* us how to use it for the first time. They *teach* us to use it if it then functions in a reinforcing way.

Two familiar autoclitics, *ought* and *should*, are used in advice. *Ought* means *owed*. "You ought to go to the Harborside Restaurant" means you owe it to yourself to go there. "You ought to serve your country" means you owe it to your country, for reasons we shall consider in a moment. *Should* is the past tense of *shall*, which has a remote etymological connection with commitment or inevitability. In other words, *ought* and *should* allude, if only indirectly, to the contingencies that reinforce taking advice.

Since we define advice by its effect on the listener, it cannot be advice when it is first given. Advice is taken first because the behavior it specifies has been reinforced in some other way. "Look out!" is perhaps first a simple mand, effective because of earlier aversive consequences. When other consequences follow, it becomes advice.

Proverbs and maxims are public advice. Etymologically, a proverb is a saying "put forth," and a maxim is a "great saying." Transmitted by books or word of mouth, they have lives of their own. They are seldom specific to the situations in which they occur and are often simply metaphors. Only a blacksmith can "strike while the iron is hot," but the expression is easily remembered and may help in advising people to act while the probability of reinforcement is high.

The Listener Is Rule-Directed

There are many reasons groups of people observe "norms," or why their members behave in "normal" ways. Some of the ways are traceable to the natural selection of the species and others to the common reinforcing environments of the members of the group. Members imitate each other and serve as models. They reinforce conformity and punish deviance. At some point in the history of a group, however, a new reason for behaving as others have behaved appears in the form of a rule. Like proverbs and maxims, rules have a life of their own apart from particular speakers or listeners. They help members of a group behave in ways most likely to be commended and least likely to be censured, and they help the group commend and censure consistently. Rules may be mands ("Don't smoke here") or composed of tacts ("Smoking is forbidden here"). A posted "No smoking" sign identifies a kind of behavior and a punitive consequence. "Black tie" on an invitation specifies the clothing to be worn to avoid criticism. The clothing worn by the military is "regulation," from the Latin *regula* or *rule*. Organizations conduct orderly meetings when their members observe rules of order. The rules tell us what we ought to do in the sense of what we owe the group. That is rather different from what we ought to do to please ourselves. The autoclitic *ought* takes on the ethical sense of what is right or normal for the group.

We "discover the meaning" of a rule when we engage in the behavior it specifies and are affected by the consequences. That is hard to do with proverbs or maxims. Having learned that "procrastination is the thief of time," we are probably no less likely to put off unpleasant tasks. Much later, when the contingencies themselves have shaped a readier completion of required work, we may discover what the maxim means, the effect it was designed to have on us.

Cognitive psychologists confuse matters by arguing that rules are *in* the contingencies and must be extracted from them. Presumably they do so because they need something to be stored according to their theories. A hungry rat presses a lever, receives food, and then begins to press more rapidly. We ourselves do something similar when exploring an unfamiliar coffee machine: we press a lever, fill our cup, and subsequently press the lever whenever a full cup has been reinforcing. Neither of us has discovered a rule; a bit of behavior has simply been reinforced. We differ from the rat, however, because we can report what has happened ("Pressing the lever produced coffee"). We can also advise others how to use the machine for the first time. We can post a rule ("Press lever to get coffee"). Only when we behave verbally in some such way, however, is a rule involved.

The rules of games describe invented contingencies of reinforcement. There are natural contingencies in which running faster than another person is reinforced, but the contingencies in a marathon are contrived. Fighting with one's fists has natural consequences in the street but additional contrived consequences in the ring. Games like baseball or basketball are played according to rules. The play is nonverbal, but the rules are maintained by umpires and referees whose behavior is decidedly verbal. The moves of go and chess are themselves verbal in the sense that they are reinforced only by their effects on the other player. The games suggest genuine conflicts—the conquest of territory in the Chinese game of go and a war between royal houses in chess, but the pieces are moved only in rule-governed ways and winning is a conventional outcome.

Although those who play games begin by following the rules, they may discover ways of playing which are not explicitly covered—new strategies in baseball and basketball, for example, or new openings and replies in go and chess. Advanced players sometimes describe these strategies in additional rules. When they do not, we call them intuitive.

Logic and mathematics presumably arose from simple contingencies of reinforcement. The distinction between *is* and *is not* and the relation of *if* to *then* are features of the physical world, and numbers must have appeared first when people started to count things. When rules were once formulated at that level, however, new rules began to be derived from them, and the practical contingencies were soon left far behind. Many mathematicians have said that what they do has no reference whatsoever to the real world, in spite of the uses made of it.

Are logic and mathematics then games? There is a distinction between *play* and *game* that is worth preserving. Games are competitive. The move made by the go or chess player who is at the moment "speaking" is reinforced by any sign that it strengthens a position against the current "listener." Skillful repertoires are shaped and maintained by such consequences. The "moves" of logicians and mathematicians are reinforced primarily by progress toward the solution of a problem. Small animals are said to play when they are behaving in ways which do not yet have any serious consequences, and logicians and mathematicians are perhaps playing in much the same sense. *Game*, however, too strongly suggests a winner and a loser.

The Listener Is Law-Governed

Rules work to the mutual advantage of those who maintain the contingencies and those who are affected by them. Rules are, in short, a form of group self-management. This can be said of the laws of governments when the governments are chosen by the governed, but it is not always the case. The so-called parliamentary laws are rules of order; they govern parliaments. The laws passed by parliaments govern nations. Special branches of a government, the police and the military, maintain the contingencies, and throughout history the contingencies have usually worked to the advantage of those who maintained them. Religious laws seem to have begun as statements about norms, but they became more than rules when supernatural sanctions were invoked in their support. What were presumably norms of the Jewish people, for example, became laws when formulated as the Ten Commandments.

Goods and services were presumably first exchanged according to evolved norms. One thing was "worth" another if it was equally reinforcing. Money as a conditioned reinforcer made it easy to compare reinforcing effects. The price posted on a loaf of bread is a rule. It describes a contingency of reinforcement ("Pay this much and take it with you"). The rules of business and industry usually become laws only when the sanctions of governments and religions are invoked. It is *illegal* or *sinful*, not unbusinesslike, to steal goods, lie about them, fail to keep promises, and so on.

The Listener Is Governed by the Laws of Science

The laws of nations and religions have been in existence for many centuries, and what it meant to be well governed must have been debated for almost as long a time, before Francis Bacon suggested that the natural world might also be governed. Its laws were, we should say now, the contingencies of reinforcement maintained by the environment. The laws of science describe those contingencies just as the laws of governments or religions describe some of the norms or rules of societies. We discover the laws of nature from experience—not, as the phenomenologists would have it, from the *appearances* of things in consciousness, in the original sense of the word *experience*, but from what has happened. Scientists improve upon experience by experimenting—by doing things to watch what happens. From both *experi*ence and *experi*ment come *experts*, those who either behave in ways that have been shaped and maintained by the contingencies or can describe them.

Science means knowledge, which is almost always thought of as a personal possession; those who possess knowledge know what to do. Behaviorally speaking, it is a possession in the sense of being a bodily state which results either from reinforcement (when the behavior is contingency-shaped) or from responding to a particular kind of verbal stimulus (when the behavior is rule-governed). If cognitive psychologists were correct in saying that rules are *in* the contingencies, it would not matter whether we learned them from the contingencies or from the rule—in other words, from acquaintance or description. The results, however, are obviously different. Those who have been directly exposed to contingencies behave more subtly and effectively than those who have merely been told, taught, or advised to behave or who follow rules. There is a difference because rules never fully describe the contingencies they are designed to replace. There is also a difference in the states of the body felt.

The latter difference has created a problem for certain philosophers of science, such as Michael Polanyi (1960) and P. W. Bridgman (1959), who insisted that the knowledge we call science must be personal. True, everything scientists now do must at least once have been contingency-shaped in someone, but most of the time scientists begin by following rules. Science is a vast verbal environment or culture.

New sciences come only from contingencies, and that was Bacon's point in his attack on the scholastics, the cognitivists of the Middle Ages. For them knowledge was rule-governed. One learned by reading books— by Aristotle, Galen, and so on. Bacon, an early experimental analyst, insisted that books follow science. Hypotheses and theories follow data. The contingencies always come first.

The Listener as Reader

The contingencies we have been reviewing are often clearest when the speaker is a writer and the listener a reader. If architecture is frozen music, then books are frozen verbal behavior. Writing leaves durable marks, and as readers we respond to durable stimuli. What is transmitted or communicated is pinned down for study. Books of travel quite obviously *tell* us what their authors have seen, heard, or read about, and books of adventure tell what they have done. Textbooks *teach* us, but only if, like programmed texts, they provide contingencies of reinforcement. A cookbook could be said to tell us something about what people eat if we are interested in the practices of a culture. It *advises* us how to make a cherry pie if we are interested in doing it. It *teaches* us to make one if the pie proves reinforcing. Games are played according to Hoyle, an early codifier of rules. Logic and mathematics are scarcely possible except in written form, and law books are no less essential to lawyers and legislators than are the tablets and bibles of religion to religious leaders. Among the tablets of science are the so-called tables of constants.

The Listener Agrees

We have been considering a kind of super-organism, the first half of which gains when the second half acts on the world, and the second half gains when the first half makes contact with that world. Those were probably the advantages that played a selective role in the evolution of verbal behavior. But when you meet someone and start to talk, you do not always tell, teach, advise, or invoke rules or laws to be followed. You converse. You talk about things both of you are familiar with. There is little to be told, taught, advised, put in order, or regulated. Speaking is reinforced when the listener tends to say more or less what the speaker says, and listening is reinforced when the speaker says more or less what the listener tends to say. Conversing is not reinforced by the consequences we have been considering but by agreement. (A conversation may even be the kind of exchange called an argument, but the point of that is to reach agreement.) To put it another way, as speakers we look for listeners, and as listeners for speakers who think as we think, where what we think is simply what we do, often covertly and verbally.

The importance of agreement is shown by the frequency with which we use autoclitics to ask about it. We say "A lovely day," and then add, "Isn't it?" or "Don't you think?" or "N'est-ce pas?" or "Nicht wahr?". We also mand agreement, as in saying, "Believe me, it was a lovely day."

As listeners or readers, we look for speakers or writers who say what we are on the point of saying. Speakers who say what we are already strongly inclined to say contribute little or nothing, and we call them boring. We listen as little as possible to speakers who say what we are not at all inclined to say (about things in which we are not interested, for example, or in terms we seldom or never use.) The speakers we like are those who help us say things we have not been quite able to say— about "the situation in Europe," for example. Much of what we prefer to hear or read is what we should have said ourselves if we had been able to do so. Unless we like to argue, we do not listen to or read those who have said things with which we have strongly disagreed.

Classical rhetoric was the art of inducing the listener to say what the speaker was saying, but often for irrelevant reasons. Many of its devices gave intraverbal or echoic support, as poetry does. A line seems just right, not because of what it says but because it scans or rhymes. Fiction with lots of conversation, and drama, which is all conversation, reinforce the reader or listener by slowly building strong operants and then offering textual or echoic stimuli to which responses can be made. You most enjoyed *Gone with the Wind* if, along with Clark Gable as Rhett

Butler, you were just ready to say, "Quite frankly, my dear, I don't give a damn." If you were not ready and wondered why Gable said it, or if you thought the remark was long overdue and were inclined to say, "Well, it's about time!", you were less likely to see the movie again sometime or recommend it to others.

The Listener and Speaker Think

All this takes on a much greater significance when the speaker and listener are the same person. The listener knows as much, in the sense of having the same history, as the teller; the listener taught knows as much as the teacher, and so on. But this does not imply that there is no need for verbal behavior. Many persons or selves reside within one skin. We imply as much when we speak of self-observation, in which one self observes another, or self-management, in which one self manages another. (See Chapter 3.) When we say that we talk to ourselves, we mean that one self talks to another. Different repertoires have been shaped and maintained by different verbal environments.

The selves may be identical except for time. We tell the same self to do something later by leaving a note. We teach a single self by rehearsing and checking our performance. We advise the same self when, for example, after an unpleasant evening, we say, "Never go there again!" We memorize maxims, rules, and laws for later use. We play solitaire or take alternating sides in a solitary game of chess. We double-check our solutions in logic and mathematics. In all this our role as listener is the important thing. We are better listeners than speakers. We were listeners before we became speakers, and we continue to listen to and read much more than we ever say or write.

Internal dialogues of this sort are most often called thinking, but all behavior is thinking, as I argue in the last chapter in *Verbal Behavior* (1957). We talk to ourselves covertly for many reasons. Occasions for overt behavior may be lacking or aversive consequences may follow if we are overheard, and so on. We also use *I think* as an autoclitic to indicate that our behavior is barely strong enough to reach the overt level. But accessibility to others is not the important distinction. When repertoires of speaker and listener come together in the same skin, things happen which are much less likely to happen when they are in separate skins. We converse with ourselves, arguing perhaps, but looking for agreement. The selves who converse have different histories (or silent verbal behavior would be useless), but they are not as different as the histories in a group discussion. Variety makes a contribution, but uniformity of background has its advantages, too. Speaker and listener speak the same language, borrow from the same sources.

Not all silent speech is of that sort. We do not always need listeners if our verbal behavior has been strongly reinforced or reinforced on an intermittent schedule. The witty response at a cocktail party occurs again and again before we go to sleep that night, and we need not ask who the listener is, any more than we need ask what the reinforcer is for every response in a scheduled performance.

Not all thinking is vocal, of course. Artists "speak" by putting paint on canvas and, as "listeners," they leave it on or take it off. They may do both covertly. Composers are both speakers and listeners, even when there are no instruments or sounds. Inventors put things together and watch how they work, either in the shop or covertly in a comfortable chair. Very little of that is likely to happen when the two repertoires are in separate skins.

This is not, of course, anything like an adequate analysis of thinking, but it moves in a promising direction. The evolution of cultures and of cultural practices has vastly extended the scope of individual behavior. The practices of the verbal environment we call a language are the greatest achievement of the human species, and verbal environments are composed of listeners.

◆ CHAPTER 5 ◆

Genes and Behavior

To say that there is a gene for a given kind of behavior or that behavior is "due to genes" does not, in the present state of genetics, mean that we can change behavior by changing genes. It means either that what an organism does responds to selective breeding or that nothing but a history of variation and selection can explain it.

I am not a field biologist, but I can give an example of the latter from personal experience. I once saw a solitary wasp prepare food for the eggs she was about to lay. She stung and paralyzed a grasshopper and then began to dig a hole in the ground some little distance away. When the grasshopper grew restless, she returned to sting it again, and when the hole was big enough, she dragged the grasshopper into it. Later, presumably after laying her eggs, she filled the hole, smoothed over the surface, and flew away. The wasp could not have learned to do any of that. Her behavior was presumably as predetermined by her genes as the pattern of her wings.

It is highly unlikely that the entire process was "due to a gene" in the sense that it appeared in that form as a single variation and was selected by its obvious consequences for the survival of the species. Simpler forms must have evolved first and have been selected by appropriate contributions to survival, the final pattern being "shaped" by a long series of contingencies of selection (Skinner, 1984).

Some features of the wasp's behavior must have been affected by incidental features of the setting. The grasshopper, the ground over which it was dragged, and the soil in which the hole was dug might all have been different. The wasp would have been prepared for such diversity if a very large repertoire of responses had evolved, one of which

49

happened to be appropriate to this particular setting. It is more likely, however, that part of the behavior of stunning, moving, and burying the grasshopper was selected by consequences that followed at the time, through the process of operant conditioning. The process appears to have evolved precisely to correct for the fact that natural selection prepares a species only for a future that fairly closely resembles the selecting past.

OPERANT CONDITIONING

The evolution of operant conditioning appears to have been accompanied by the evolution of susceptibilities to reinforcement. A young duckling, for example, not only shows an innate tendency to follow a large moving object (of which the commonest will be its mother); it is also susceptible to reinforcement by any reduction in the distance between itself and such an object, as Peterson (1960) has shown. (Imprinting is apparently a different process.)

Although the evolution of behavior remains largely a matter of inference, operant conditioning is studied experimentally, and complex repertoires of behavior are shaped and maintained in strength with appropriate contingencies of reinforcement. Once the process of shaping has been recognized, behavior once attributed to feelings and states of mind can be traced to simpler and more readily identified sources. Donald R. Griffin (1984) has argued, for example, that chimpanzees show consciousness and intentional thought when they fashion sticks to collect termites and, if that is the case, that we must say the same thing for the assassin bug, which collects termites in an even more complex way. "Perhaps," Griffin (p. 459) says, "we should be ready to infer conscious thinking whenever any animal shows such ingenious behavior, regardless of its taxonomic group and our preconceived notions about limitations of animal consciousness." But if comparable behavior can be shaped with contrived contingencies of reinforcement, it could have been shaped and maintained by natural selection. We have no more reason to say that an individual designs its own behavior than to say that a species does, and no more reason to say that a species designs its behavior than that it designs the nerves and muscles with which the behavior is executed.

Behavior due primarily to operant conditioning can be traced to genes only by way of a process operating during the lifetime of the individual. The state of the brain due to reinforcement may resemble the state due to natural selection (the observed behaviors can be indistinguishable), but one is due to a gene, in the sense of being explained by natural selection, while the other is due to reinforcement during the lifetime of the individual, and hence, it must also be due, in part, to the genes responsible for operant conditioning. Genes responsible for the uncommitted behavior from which operants are drawn and for the susceptibilities to reinforcement which make consequences strengthening also need to be identified. (The role of operant conditioning is too important to dismiss simply as "epigenesis.")

SOCIAL BEHAVIOR

The pathway back to genes can be even more devious. An organism cannot acquire a large repertoire of behavior through operant conditioning alone in a nonsocial environment. Other organisms are important. A tendency to imitate presumably evolved because doing what another organism was doing frequently made a similar contribution to survival. When one member of a grazing herd sees an approaching predator and runs, others who run also improve their chances of escaping, although they have not seen the predator. Once imitation has evolved, contingencies prevail for the evolution of modeling. If, for example, young birds learn to fly sooner when they imitate their parents, they are more likely to survive if the parents fly in conspicuous, easily imitated ways. The evolution of audible signaling (calls, cries, and so on) was a further advance.

Operant behavior is imitated because the same *reinforcing* consequences are likely to follow. The imitation is important because it "primes" behavior in the sense of bringing it out for the first time. Reinforcing consequences may then take over. Imitation is especially important when the contingencies are rare. In an example that has recently attracted attention, birds learned to peck through the foil caps of milk bottles. Presumably the behavior of one bird had been adventitiously reinforced under especially favorable circumstances, and other birds then imitated it. (Too much is read into both phylogenic and ontogenic imitation when it is called "observational learning.") There seems to be no evidence that the birds modeled the behavior, that is, showed other birds what to do to get at the milk.

Operant behavior can be called modeling only when the behavior of the imitator has reinforcing consequences for the modeler. For example, parents model behavior because the children who imitate them thus need less care or can serve as helpers. That is a deferred consequence, however, which requires special mediation. The mediation seems to require an additional process, which came into existence when an evolutionary change brought the vocal musculature of the human species under operant control. That led to the evolution of verbal behavior, which is different from, and much more extensive than, phylogenic vocal signaling.

People prime behavior by telling each other what to do as well as by showing them. Because verbal behavior has no effect on the physical environment and depends on reinforcement through the mediation of other people, the route "back to genes" is still more devious.

CULTURE

What anthropologists have to say about a culture is not always helpful. For structuralists, a culture is what people do or what they may have done as the culture "developed." There is little or no interest in the origins of the behavior. Defining a culture as the ideas and values of a group is more meaningful if "ideas" refer to what people do and "values" to the consequences that have induced them to do it, although the references remain vague. A culture can be more usefully defined as the contingencies of reinforcement maintained by a group. The contingencies shape the behavior of the members of the group and are transmitted when newly shaped members join in the shaping of others. If the group is confined to a particular part of the world, some characteristic contingencies may be physical, but most will be social.

As social environments, cultures evolve through a third kind of variation and selection. Consider another example of social behavior that has recently attracted attention. A monkey accidentally dips a sweet potato into sea water, and the resulting salted, grit-free potato is especially reinforcing. Dipping is therefore repeated and becomes a standard part of the monkey's repertoire. Other monkeys then imitate the behavior and come under the control of the same contingencies. Eventually, all the monkeys on a given island wash their sweet potatoes. Washing would usually be called a cultural practice, particularly if on another island a similar accidental reinforcement had never occurred and the monkeys never washed their sweet potatoes.

The survival of a culture is more than a product of contingencies of reinforcement, however. It occurs when practices contribute to the survival of the practicing group and survive with the group. If, for example, washing sweet potatoes prevented the spread of a fatal disease, the resulting contribution to the survival of the group would not be a reinforcing consequence.

Some practices said to be characteristic of a culture lie beyond showing and telling. One person modifies the behavior of another, for example, by arranging contingencies of reinforcement. The first reinforcers used in that way were probably negative. Stronger members of a group could impose aversive conditions from which weaker members would escape by acting in ways that worked to the advantage of the stronger members. Positive reinforcement presumably came later as a practice because its effects are at least slightly delayed and hence less likely to shape behavior.

The distinction is harder to see when survival more closely resembles reinforcement. Governments, for example, operate by maintaining contingencies of (usually) negative reinforcement. Citizens obey the law to escape from or avoid fines and imprisonment. Laws are maintained primarily because the consequences reinforce the behavior of those who compose the government and maintain them. If those who have the power to maintain the laws abuse their power, however, they may generate escape (defection) or attack (revolution). If some sort of equilibrium is reached, both parties enjoy some measure of security or order. Security and order are often called the *justifications* of government. They contribute to the survival of the group and hence of the practice, but they are not reinforcing consequences, either for governors or governed.

Practices involving positive reinforcement have similar by-products, which also function in a third type of selection. Those who possess goods can use them to reinforce behavior that produces more goods. Excessive use may lead to countercontrol in the form of strikes or boycotts. If some kind of equilibrium is maintained, everyone may enjoy the possession of a reasonable quantity of goods. But that "justification" of the practice is not contingent on behavior in such a way as to function as a reinforcer.

Practices emerging from either positive or negative reinforcement could be said to serve as variations. Some of them are then selected by the survival of the practicing group. Other consequences contributing to the survival of a culture are less like the consequences responsible for the practices. Thus, practical contingencies lead individuals to ask each other questions that result in the self-observation we call being conscious; other questions generate the behavior of self-management we call thinking. Together, these lead to science.

Just as it has taken a long time to discover that "the organism is the servant of the gene," so it has taken a long time to discover that the individual is the servant of the culture, and that it is the culture that eventually survives or perishes. (Perhaps we have now come full circle and are beginning to understand that the ultimate question is still the survival of the species.)

Lumsden and Wilson (1981) speak of a linkage between biological and cultural evolution. "Coevolution," they say, "is a complicated, fascinating interaction in which culture is generated and shaped by biological imperatives while biological properties are simultaneously altered by genetic evolution in response to cultural history" (p. 1). But have *homo sapiens* and human cultures evolved at the same time? Imitation and modeling are shared by other species, but a large part of human culture is due to verbal behavior. Because no other species has acquired operant control of the vocal musculature, it must have appeared very late, when human genetics had reached essentially its present state. Very little genetic change can have occurred "in response to cultural history." Most of science and technology, for example, has evolved during the past 2,500 years. Must we suppose that Aristotle would have had trouble understanding it? Religion, government, and literature have taken longer, but not very much longer as natural selection goes. In other words, almost all cultural practices appear to have evolved after the species had reached essentially its present genetic condition. Little or no coevolution was possible.

MISUNDERSTANDINGS

As a narrative account of what a species, person, or culture has done, the term *history* makes perhaps the fewest commitments. *Evolution* and *development* go further. To evolve first meant to unroll, as in unrolling a scroll; to *develop* once meant to unfold, as in opening a letter. Both meant to disclose something that was already there. It was known before Darwin, of course, that species had changed, although presumably according to a plan. Developmental psychologists follow the unrolling or unfolding of behavior as children grow older. A child may be "trained," in the horticultural sense of guided during growth, but the essentials of what eventually appears are in some way predetermined. Social theorists such as Hegel and Marx and some anthropologists have argued that cultures must also pass through a fixed order of stages. These are all essentially creationist views. What happens is said to be due to the original nature of species, person, or society and therefore somehow "due to genes." The path to genes is more devious, however, when natural selection, operant conditioning, and the evolution of cultural practices are taken severally into account.

Similarities among the three levels of selection have often proved misleading. In what sense, for example, can we speak of the "social life" of insects? Individuals in a colony of ants respond to each other differently than people respond to each other in human society. In a colony the behavior is "released" in ways determined by natural selection. In a human society the behavior is largely the product of operant conditioning under social contingencies maintained by a culture.

To speak of the "language of bees" is to risk a similar misunderstanding. A bee does not really dance to "tell" other bees where nectar and pollen can be found. (Dancing has been selected when other bees have more readily found them, no current consequences playing any part.) Nor do other bees respond to the dance because of what they "learn" about the location of nectar and pollen. (Their responses have been selected when they have more readily discovered nectar, that consequence having no current effect.) Dancing resembles speaking, and responding to a dance resembles listening, but speaking and listening have a different origin. They are shaped and maintained by a verbal environment.

It is particularly easy to be misled when the effects of contingencies of selection are treated as traits of character. For example, are there altruistic and aggressive genes? If we say that behavior is altruistic if it helps another person while harming the helper and aggressive if it harms another person while helping the harmer, there are examples at all three levels of selection. Natural selection presumably explains why a male insect copulates and then dies and why a lion kills and eats a gazelle. Operant conditioning presumably explains why a mother allays her child's hunger by giving it food while going hungry herself and why a mugger steals a handbag. The evolution of a culture presumably explains why soldiers die for their country and why one country ravages another. (It is sometimes argued that behavior should be called aggressive only when positive consequences are lacking: the lion must kill and not eat, the mugger must already have plenty of money, and the country must have no need for space or material, but that is only to appeal to unidentified variables among which the same three levels could presumably be distinguished.) It might be argued that altruism as a genetic trait merely makes it more *likely* that a mother will help her child or soldiers die for their country and that aggression as a genetic trait merely makes a mugger more likely to mug or one government to invade another. Even so, similarities of the behaviors from which we infer the traits can still obscure differences in the controlling variables.

Contributions by genes have also been inferred from the fact that all cultures have common features. All languages, for example, seem to show universal rules of grammar, and Chomsky (1980), among others, has argued that children must be born with knowledge of the rules. Such universals derive, however, from common features of the social environments that generate verbal behavior: for example, in all languages people call each other by name, ask questions, give orders, and name objects.

Similarly, it has been argued that all cultures have gods and that there must therefore be a "gene for religion." But social environments share certain practices. People ask for help and, when in great need, do so when there is no one to ask. People thank those responsible for their good fortune and, when particularly fortunate, do so when there is no one to thank. A god is one answer to the question, "Whom are you asking or thanking?" and is most often fashioned significantly after one of those most often asked and thanked—a king, lord, father, or mother.

Sociobiology was not first in saying that human traits are "due to genes." An earlier movement, psychobiology, argued that feelings and states of mind were conditions of the nervous system. A sensation, for example, was a state of the brain, which was due in turn to genes. When human behavior is analyzed in its own right as a function of environmental variables, however, rather than as the expression of feelings and states of mind, the nervous system is seen to play a different role. Behavioral scientists observe three things: the action of the environment on an organism, the action of the organism on the environment, and changes which then follow. There are gaps in that account which only neurologists will eventually fill with their different instruments and techniques. Brain processes are not another "aspect" of behavior; they are another part of what an organism does. The whole story will eventually be told by the joint action of the sciences of genetics, behavior, and culture.

◆ PART TWO ◆

Professional Issues

◆ CHAPTER 6 ◆

Whatever Happened to Psychology as the Science of Behavior?

There can scarcely be anything more familiar than human behavior. We are always in the presence of at least one behaving person. Nor can there be anything more important, whether it is our own behavior or that of those whom we see every day or who are responsible for what is happening in the world at large. Nevertheless human behavior is certainly not the thing we understand best. Granted that it is possibly the most difficult subject ever submitted to scientific analysis, it is still puzzling that so little has been done with the instruments and methods which have been so productive in the other sciences. Perhaps what is wrong is that behavior has seldom been thought of as a subject matter in its own right but rather as the mere expression or symptom of more important happenings inside the behaving person.

The Homeric Greeks thought they knew the very organs. The *thumos,* or heart, was one of them. It was a vital organ (when it stopped, the person died), but for the Greeks it was also the seat of such things as hunger, joy, fear, will, and thought. To be undecided about something, for example, was to have a divided *thumos.* We may smile at that, but we do much the same thing ourselves. Here are some of the definitions of the word *heart* in Webster's *Third New International Dictionary* (1981): *the whole personality* ("deep in one's heart"), *intelligence* ("knowing something by heart"), *character* ("look into the heart of a person"), *compassion* ("have a heart"), *mood* ("a heavy heart"), *opinion* ("a change of heart"), *affection* ("a broken heart"), *goodwill* ("with all my heart"), *courage* ("a stout heart"), and *taste* ("a man after one's own heart"). Of course, we do not mean the real heart, but the Greeks may not have done so either. The point is that, like them, we appeal to something inside a person to explain what that person does.

When Galen described human anatomy in greater detail, especially the nerves connecting the brain with sense organs and muscles, it was clear that the Greeks had got the wrong organ. They should have said brain. It was Descartes who showed how brain and nerves could explain the kind of behavior which was later called reflex. Although the notion of a stimulus suggested an external cause, the search for internal causes did not stop. During the 19th and early 20th centuries reflexes were studied by physiologists. Sherrington's book was called *The Integrative Action of the Nervous System* (1906) and Pavlov's had the subtitle *The Physiological Activity of the Cerebral Cortex* (1927).

It was hard to find plausible organs for many kinds of behavior, of course, and Plato and others gave up the attempt. Speculation could then be freer. Although we think we see the object we are looking at, for example, it was said that we must see only an internal copy of it, since we can still see it with our eyes closed and even recall it from memory later on. Before we act, moreover, we can merely think of acting; we can have intentions, expectations, or ideas and do nothing more about them. Somewhere inside the body, in short, there seemed to be another person who is made of a different kind of stuff. For 2,500 years philosophers and, later, psychologists have discussed the nature of that stuff, but for our present purposes we may accept *Punch's* (1855) famous dismissal:

What is Matter?—Never mind.
What is Mind?—No matter.

Mind or matter, it was something *inside* a person that determined what that person did.

EARLY BEHAVIORISM

The theory of evolution raised a different question about those internal causes. Nonhuman animals had reflexes and organs, but did they have minds? Darwin, committed to the continuity of species, said yes, and he and his contemporaries could cite examples which seemed to prove him right. It was Lloyd Morgan who objected that the examples could be explained in other ways and Watson who took the inevitable next step and contended that the same thing could be said of human animals. An early form of behaviorism was born.

The predilection for internal causes survived, however. Probably as a reaction to the heavily mentalistic psychology of the time, a central issue in early behaviorism was the existence of consciousness. Experiments were designed to show that animals either could or could not do everything traditionally attributed to feelings and states of mind. If they could not, something like a mental life would have to be recognized. Perhaps because Watson first studied instincts, he replaced feelings and states of mind with habits. He may have meant nothing more than the behavior said to show the presence of instincts and habits, but he turned later to conditioned reflexes, and his associate, Lashley, went still further into the nervous system. Later, Tolman restored purpose to the organism and, still later, installed cognitive maps and hypotheses. Clark Hull built an elaborate system of internal processes which, as in "Afferent neural interaction," for example, became increasingly physiological. In short, 3,000 years after the Homeric Greeks, mentalistic and behavioristic psychologists alike were still looking inside the organism for explanations of its behavior. To say that the habit of doing so must have been deeply ingrained would be to give another example.

RADICAL BEHAVIORISM

Behavior seems to have been first accepted as a subject matter in its own right when organisms were studied which were too small, and their behavior too simple, to suggest internal initiating processes. H. S. Jennings' *The Behavior of the Lower Organisms* (1906) was the great classic, of course, but more to the point were the work and theories of Jacques Loeb (1916). Loeb's formulation of tropisms and his emphasis on "forced movement" dispensed with internal explanations. The thing to be studied was the behavior of the "organism as a whole." And that could be said of larger organisms, as well.

Equally important were new developments in the philosophy of science. Concepts began to be more carefully defined in terms of the operations from which they were inferred. Ernst Mach, especially with his *Science of Mechanics* (1915), was an important figure. Later P. W. Bridgman took a similar line in his *Logic of Modern Physics* (1928). In *Philosophy* (1927), a book said to have been written as a potboiler, Bertrand Russell anticipated the logical positivists by several years and "behavioristically considered" a number of psychological terms. My thesis, "The concept of the reflex in the description of behavior" (1931), was in that tradition. A reflex, I argued, was not something that happened inside the organism; it was a law of behavior. All we actually observed was that a response was a function of a stimulus. It could also be a function of variables in the fields of conditioning, motivation, and emotion, but they too were outside the organism. I called them "third variables," but Tolman later put them back inside and called them "intervening."

It was easy to make my case because reflexes, conditioned or unconditioned, were only a small part of the behavior of more complex organisms. The research I was doing at the time, however, had a broader scope: the environment not only triggered behavior, it selected it. Consequences seemed, indeed, to be more important than antecedents. Their role had, of course, long been recognized—for example, as reward or punishment. It was Thorndike (1898) who first studied their effects experimentally. Given several possible ways of solving a problem, a cat eventually took the successful one when incorrect ways, or "errors," dropped out.

I studied the same process in a different way. Prompted by Pavlov's emphasis on the control of conditions, I made sure that all Thorndike's "errors" were eliminated before a successful response could be made. A single "reinforcing" consequence was then enough; the response was immediately and rapidly repeated. I called the process operant conditioning. Thorndike had attributed his effect to feelings of satisfaction and annoyance, which were inside the organism, of course, but I traced the strengthening effect of an operant reinforcer to its survival value in the natural selection of the species.

My first arrangement of setting, response, and consequence was quite simple, but I reported the effects of more complex "contingencies of reinforcement" in *The Behavior of Organisms* (1938). Still more elaborate ones have been studied for more than 50 years in laboratories throughout the world. Most of the work has been done with nonhuman animals to cover a wider range of conditions than would be feasible with human subjects and to avoid "verbal contamination."

The contamination has also been studied, however. Verbal behavior differs from nonverbal in certain features of the contingencies of reinforcement. The verbal stimuli we call advice, rules, or laws describe or allude to contingencies of reinforcement. People who have been advised or who follow rules and obey laws behave for either of two very different reasons: their behavior has been directly reinforced by its consequences or they are responding to descriptions of contingencies. How and why they respond to descriptions is explained by analyzing verbal contingencies of reinforcement.

A better understanding of verbal contingencies has also brought two important fields of psychology within range of an operant analysis. One of them is self-observation. The analysis does not "ignore consciousness" or bring it back into a behavioral science; it simply analyzes the way in which verbal contingencies of reinforcement bring *private* events into control of the behavior called introspecting. Only when we are asked about what we have done, are doing, or are about to do, or why, have we any reason to observe or recall our behavior or its controlling variables. All behavior, human and nonhuman, is unconscious; it becomes "conscious" when verbal environments provide the contingencies necessary for self-observation. (It is the person, of course, who is "conscious" or "unconscious," not the behavior.) Other verbal contingencies generate the behavior called self-management or thinking, in which problems are solved by manipulating either contingencies (as in practical problem solving) or rules (as in "reasoning").

Much of this is at the moment only an interpretation, but that is a common scientific practice. Astronomers interpret the waves and particles reaching Earth from outer space by using what has been learned under controllable conditions in the laboratory—for example, in high energy physics. In a similar way we use what has been learned from an experimental analysis to explain behavior which cannot, at the moment at least, be brought under experimental control, such as covert behavior or behavior observed casually in daily life.

The traditional preoccupation with internal explanatory agents breaks behavior into fragments. Psychophysicists, for example, study the effects of stimuli, but only up to the point at which they are supposedly received by an inner agent. Psycholinguists record changes in the number of words or the length of sentences a child speaks over a period of time, but usually with no record of what happened when the child heard similar words or sentences or of what consequences followed when they were spoken. Psychologists study verbal learning by asking their subjects to memorize and recall nonsense syllables, but the word *nonsense* makes it clear that they are not interested in all the variables controlling the behavior. Somehow the internal entity or process acts as a starting or stopping place. A bit of sensing is studied by one psychologist, a bit of behaving by another, and a bit of changing by still another. The experimental analysis of behavior puts Humpty Dumpty together again by studying relatively complete episodes, each with a history of reinforcement, a current setting, a response, and a reinforcing consequence.

Many of the facts, and even some of the principles, which psychologists have discovered when they may have thought they were discovering something else are useful. We can accept, for example, what psychophysicists tell us about responses to stimuli without agreeing that they show a mathematical relation between mental and physical worlds. We can accept many of the facts reported by cognitive psychologists without believing that their subjects were processing information or storing representations or rules. We can accept what happened when subjects responded to descriptions of contingencies of reinforcement without believing that they were "subjectively evaluating expected utilities."

The relation between an analysis of behavior as such and physiology is quite simple. Each of these sciences has instruments and methods appropriate to part of a behavioral episode. Gaps are inevitable in a behavioral account. Stimulus and response are separated in time and space, for example, and so are a reinforcement on one day and stronger behavior on the next. The gaps can be filled only with the instruments and methods of physiology. They cannot be filled by introspection, because there are no sensory nerves going to the right parts of the brain.

For more than half a century the experimental analysis of behavior as a function of environmental variables and the use of that analysis in the interpretation and modification of behavior in the world at large have reached into every field of traditional psychology. Yet they have not *become* psychology, and the question is, Why not? Perhaps one answer is to be found in three formidable obstacles which have stood in their path.

Obstacle I: Humanistic Psychology

Many people find the implications of a behavioral analysis disturbing because the traditional direction of action of organism and environment seems to be reversed. Instead of saying that the organism sees, attends to, perceives, "processes," or otherwise acts upon stimuli, an operant analysis holds that stimuli acquire control of behavior through the part they play in contingencies of reinforcement. Instead of saying that an organism stores copies of the contingencies to which it is exposed and later retrieves and responds to them again, it says that the organism is changed by the contingencies and later responds as a changed organism, the contingencies having passed into history. The environment takes over the control formerly assigned to an internal, originating agent.

Some long-admired features of human behavior are then threatened. Following the lead of evolutionary theory, an operant analysis replaces creation with variation and selection. There is no longer any need for a creative mind or plan, or for purpose or goal-direction. Just as we do not say that species-specific behavior evolved *in order that* a species could adapt to the environment but evolved *when* it adapted, so we say that operant behavior is not strengthened by reinforcement *in order that* the individual can adjust to the environment but is strengthened *when* the individual adjusts (where *adapt* and *adjust* mean "behave effectively with respect to").

The disenthronement of a creator also seems to threaten personal freedom (can we be free if the environment is in control?) and personal worth (can we take credit for our achievements if they are nothing more than the effects of circumstances?). Behavioral analysis also seems to threaten ethical, religious, and governmental systems which hold people responsible for their conduct. Who or what is responsible if unethical, immoral, or illegal behavior is due to heredity or personal history? Humanistic psychologists have attacked behavioral science along these lines. Like creationists in their attack on secular humanists (with the humanism on the other side), humanistic psychologists often challenge the content or selection of textbooks, the appointment of teachers and administrators, the design of curricula, and the allocation of funds.

Obstacle II: Psychotherapy

Certain exigencies of the helping professions are another obstacle in the path of a scientific analysis. Psychotherapists must talk with their clients and, with rare exceptions, do so in everyday English, which is heavily laden with references to internal causes—"I ate because I was *hungry*," "I did it because I *knew* how to do it," and so on. All fields of science tend to have two languages, of course. Scientists speak one with casual acquaintances and the other with colleagues. In a relatively young science, such as psychology, the use of the vernacular may be challenged. How often have behaviorists heard, "You just said, 'It crossed my mind." I thought there wasn't supposed to be any mind." It has been a long time since anyone has challenged a physicist who said, "That desk is made of solid oak," by protesting, "But I thought you said that matter was mostly empty space."

The two languages of psychology raise a special problem. What we feel when we are hungry and when we know how to do something are states of our bodies, but we do not have very good ways of observing them, and those who teach us to observe them usually have no way at all. We were taught to say, "I'm hungry," for example, by persons who knew perhaps only that we had not eaten for some time ("You missed your lunch; you must be *hungry*.") or had observed something about our behavior ("You are eating ravenously. You must be *hungry*."). Similarly, we were taught to say "I know" by persons who had perhaps only seen us doing something ("Oh, you *know* how to do that!") or had told us how to do something and then said, "Now you *know*." The trouble is that private states are almost always poorly correlated with the public evidence.

References to private events are, nevertheless, often accurate enough to be useful. If we are preparing a meal for a friend, we are not likely to ask, "How long has it been since you last ate?" or "Will you probably eat a great deal?" We simply ask, "How *hungry* are you?" If a friend is driving us to an appointment, we are not likely to ask, "Have you driven there before?" or "Has anyone told you where it is?" Instead we ask, "Do you *know* where it is?" Being hungry and knowing where something is are states of the body resulting from personal histories, and what is said about them may be the only available evidence of those histories. Nevertheless, how much a person eats does depend on a history of deprivation, not on how a deprived body feels; and whether a person reaches a given destination does depend on whether he or she has driven there before or has been told how to get there, not on introspective evidence of the effects.

Psychotherapists must ask people what has happened to them and how they feel because the confidential relationship of therapist and client prevents direct inquiry. (It is sometimes argued that what a person remembers may be more important than what actually happened, but that is true only if something else has happened, in which case independent evidence would be better to have.) But although the use of reports of feelings and states of mind can be justified on practical grounds, their use cannot be justified in theory making. The temptation, however, is great. Psychoanalysts, for example, specialize in feelings. Instead of investigating the early lives of their patients or watching them with their families, friends, or business associates, they ask them what has happened and how they feel about it. It is not surprising that they should then construct theories in terms of memories, feelings, and states of mind, or that they should say that an analysis of behavior in terms of environmental events lacks "depth."

Obstacle III: Cognitive Psychology

A graph showing the frequency of the appearance of the word *cognitive* in the psychological literature would be interesting. An increase in frequency could probably first be seen around 1960; the subsequent acceleration would be exponential. Is there any field of psychology today in which something does not seem to be gained by adding that charming adjective to the occasional noun? The popularity may not be hard to explain. When we became psychologists, we learned new ways of talking about human behavior. If the new ways were "behavioristic," they were not very much like the old ways. The old terms were taboo, and eyebrows were raised when we used them. But when certain developments seemed to show that the old ways might be right after all, everyone could relax. Mind was back.

Information theory was one of those developments, computer technology another. Troublesome problems seemed to vanish like magic.

A detailed study of sensation and perception was no longer needed; one could simply speak of processing information. It was no longer necessary to construct settings in which to observe behavior; one could simply describe them. Rather than observe what people actually did, one could simply ask them what they would probably do.

That mentalistic psychologists are uneasy about these uses of introspection is clear from the desperation with which they are turning to brain science, asking it to tell them what perceptions, feelings, ideas, and intentions "really are." Brain scientists are happy to accept the assignment. To complete the account of an episode of behavior (for example, to explain what happens when a reinforcement brings an organism under the control of a given stimulus) is not only beyond the present range of brain science, it would lack the glamour of a revelation about the nature of mind. But psychology may find it dangerous to turn to neurology for help. Once you tell the world that another science will explain what your key terms really mean, you must forgive the world if it decides that the other science is doing the important work.

Cognitive psychologists like to say that "the mind is what the brain does," but surely the rest of the body plays a part. The mind is what the *body* does. It is what the *person* does. In other words, it *is* the behavior, and that is what behaviorists have been saying for more than half a century. To focus on an organ is to rejoin the Homeric Greeks.

Cognitive psychologists and brain scientists have united to form a new discipline called cognitive science. It is enormously appealing. From a single page in a book review titled "Inside the Thinking Animal," in the *New York Times* (Restak, 1985), we learn that the separation of mind and brain, as represented by the separation of psychiatry and neurology, is now blurring, that biochemistry will tell us about depression, that in dreams information is processed very differently from in the waking state, that cognitive neuroscientists would not explain forgetting a friend's name as repression but as a breakdown of memory retrieval, that psychoanalysis was a precursor to current developments in the neuro-sciences, and that quantum physics offers the most satisfying answer to understanding the mind and brain relationship and the nature of reality itself. Very rich fare, indeed, until one counts the calories. The bodily state felt as depression will no doubt *eventually* be understood by biochemists (it is now being changed with the biochemicals we call drugs). Dreaming is no doubt different from the waking state, but whether information is "processed" in either state is still a question. Is there any difference between "forgetting" and "failing to retrieve a memory," except the gratuitous metaphor in the latter expression? Is it likely that neurology will eventually find the elaborate "mental apparatus" of psychoanalysis? And must we wait for quantum physics before saying anything useful about the mind-brain relationship, let alone reality itself?

A preference for rule-governed rather than contingency-shaped behavior explains the warmth with which cognitive psychologists have also welcomed artificial intelligence. The artificial organisms which show artificial intelligence are much more complex than the automata which inspired the reflex theory of Descartes, but both do only what they are told to do. Fairly simple models have been built which are changed by the consequences of their behavior, and they are much more like real organisms, but cognitive psychologists naturally prefer those which follow rules, including rules for deriving new rules from old. Logicians and mathematicians have been discovering, composing, and testing rules of the latter sort for centuries. Machines can do some of the work and, like a hand calculator, do it much faster. Mathematicians and logicians have never given very consistent accounts of how they work, in part because they have tried to discover their "thought processes." If an artificial organism could be designed to do what logicians and mathematicians do, or even more than they have ever done, it will be the best evidence we have that intuitive mathematical and logical thinking is only following rules, no matter how obscure. And following a rule is behaving.

DAMAGE AND REPAIR

By their very nature, the anti-science stance of humanistic psychology, the practical exigencies of the helping professions, and the cognitive restoration of the Royal House of Mind have worked against the definition of psychology as the science of behavior. Perhaps that could be justified if something more valuable had been achieved, but has that happened? Is there a better conception of psychology? To judge from the psychological literature, there are either many conceptions, largely incompatible, or no clear conception at all. Introductory textbooks do not help because, with an eye on adoptions, the authors call their subject the "science of behavior *and* mental life" and make sure that every field of interest is covered. What the public learns from the media is no more helpful.

Is there a rapidly expanding body of facts and principles? Of our three obstacles, only cognitive psychology offers itself as an experimental science. It usually does so with a certain éclat, but have its promises been kept? When the journal *Psychology Today* celebrated its 15th anniversary, it asked 10 psychologists to name the most important discoveries made during that period of time. As Nicolas Wade (1982) has pointed out, no 2 of the 10 agreed on a single achievement that could properly be called psychology. For more than two years *Science* has not published a single paper on psychology, except one on memory that cited work on brain-operated and brain-damaged people and one on the neurological basis of memory retrieval. Apparently the editors of *Science* no longer regard psychology itself as a member of the scientific community.

Nor has psychology developed a strong technology. Internal determiners get in the way of effective action. A paper on "Energy conservation behavior" (Costanzo, Archer, Aronson, & Pettigrew, 1986) in the *American Psychologist* carries the significant subtitle, "The difficult path from information to action." If we take the "rational-economic" path and tell people about the consequences of what they are doing or of what they might do instead, they are not likely to change. (And for good reason: information is not enough; people seldom take advice unless taking other advice has been reinforced.) If, on the other hand, we adopt the "attitude-change" approach, people are also not likely to change. Attitudes are inferences from the behavior that is said to show their presence and are not directly accessible. If I turn off unnecessary lights and appliances in my home, it is not because I have a "positive attitude" toward conservation, but because doing so has had some kind of reinforcing consequence. To induce people to conserve energy, one must change contingencies of reinforcement, not attitudes. No one should try to beat a "path from information to action," because action is the problem and contingencies are the solution.

Unable to offer a useful conception of its subject matter, psychology has not formed good relations with other sciences. As we have seen, it has given neurologists an impossible assignment, and the search for internal determiners has obscured any help it could give genetics. Once you have formed the noun *ability* from the adjective *able*, you are in trouble. Aqua regia has the *ability* to dissolve gold; but chemists will not look for an ability, they will look for atomic and molecular processes. Much of the controversy about the heritability of intelligence, schizophrenia, delinquency, and so on is due to the conceptualization of abilities and traits of character as explanatory entities. Longevity is a "heritable trait," but rather than try to assign it to a gene, geneticists will look at processes which contribute to a long life. The genetics of behavior can be much more directly studied by interbreeding members of a species which behave in different ways under the controlled conditions of the laboratory.

Psychology gives very little help to the behavioral sciences—sociology, anthropology, linguistics, political science, and economics. They have their own technical vocabularies, but beyond them, except for brief flirtations with utilitarianism, Marxism, psychoanalysis, and the like, they have used the vernacular, with all its references to internal causes. Their data are usually more objective than those of psychology, but hypothetical explanations still flourish.

Beyond the current reach of all the sciences lies an issue that cannot be safely neglected by any of them—the future of the world. For a variety of reasons all three of our "obstacles" have had special reasons for neglecting this future. Humanistic psychologists are unwilling to sacrifice feelings of freedom and worth for the sake of a future, and when cognitive psychologists turn to feelings and states of mind for theoretical purposes and psychotherapists for practical ones, they emphasize the here and now. Behavior modification, in contrast, is more often preventive than remedial. In both instruction and therapy, current reinforcers (often contrived) are arranged to strengthen behavior which student and client will find useful *in the future*.

When Gandhi was asked, "What are we to do?" he is said to have replied, "Think of the poorest man you have ever met and then ask if what you are doing is of any benefit to him." But he must have meant "of any benefit to the many people who, without your help, will be like him." To feed the hungry and clothe the naked are remedial acts. We can easily see what is wrong and what needs to be done. It is much harder to see and do something about the fact that world agriculture must feed and clothe billions of people, most of them yet unborn. It is not enough to *advise* people how to behave in ways which will make a future for the species possible; they must be given effective reasons for behaving in those ways, and that means effective contingencies of reinforcement.

Unfortunately, references to feelings and states of mind have an emotional appeal which behavioral alternatives usually lack. Here is an example: "If the world is to be saved, people must learn to be noble without being cruel, to be filled with faith, yet open to truth, to be inspired by great purposes without hating those who thwart them." That is an "inspiring" sentence. We like nobility, faith, truth, and great purposes and dislike cruelty and hatred. But what does it inspire us to *do*? What must be changed if people are to behave in noble rather than cruel ways, to accept the word of others but never without questioning it, to do things that have consequences too remote to serve as reinforcers, and to refrain from attacking those who oppose them? The fault, dear Brutus, is not in our stars *nor in ourselves* that we are underlings. The fault is in our world. It is a world that we have made and one that we must change if the species is to survive.

For at least 3,000 years philosophers and psychologists have proceeded on the assumption that because they were themselves behaving organisms, they had privileged access to the causes of their behavior. But has any introspectively observed feeling or state of mind yet been unambiguously identified in either mental or physical terms? Has any ability or trait of character been statistically established to the satisfaction of everyone? Do we know how anxiety changes intention, how memories alter decisions, how intelligence changes emotion, and so on? And, of course, has anyone ever satisfactorily explained how the mind acts on the body or the body on the mind?

Questions of this sort should never have been asked. Psychology has much to gain by confining itself to its accessible subject matter and leaving the rest of the story to physiology.

◆ CHAPTER 7 ◆

The Operant Side of Behavior Therapy

In 1913 John B. Watson issued his famous manifesto: The subject matter of psychology was behavior. It is easy to forget how radical that must have seemed. Psychology had always been the science of mental life, and that life was to be studied through introspection, a process of self-examination borrowed from the philosophers, who had used it for more than 2,000 years. People were said to behave in given ways because of what they were feeling or thinking, and feelings and thoughts were therefore the things to study. If animals sometimes behaved rather like people, they probably had feelings and some kind of mental life, although they might not know that they had.

Seventy-five years have seen a great change. Introspection has been returned to the philosophers. There are no longer any "trained observers" in the Wundtian tradition, and cognitive psychologists no longer observe the mental processes they talk about. The processes are hypotheses, to be confirmed either by inferences from the behavior they are said to explain or by a different kind of observation, of the nervous system.

Meanwhile, two flourishing sciences of behavior have appeared. Ethology is one of them. The behavior of animals in a natural environment is no longer explained by imagining what the animals are feeling or thinking but by the contributions the behavior may have made to the future of their genes. In the other science, the experimental analysis of behavior, animals are observed in the laboratory, where many of the conditions of which their behavior is a function can be controlled. Most of the behavior is traced to operant reinforcement, a different kind of selective consequence acting during the lifetime of the individual.

As more and more of the variables of which behavior is a function are identified and their role analyzed, less remains to be explained in mentalistic ways. There are proportionate gains in the application of the analysis. It has always been difficult to do very much with feelings and states of mind because of their inaccessibility. The environmental variables are often within reach.

Contact between the basic analysis and its applications is important. Although new facts often turn up in the course of applying a science, the science itself usually moves more rapidly into new territory. In what follows I review some well-known practices in behavior therapy from the point of view of behavior analysis and discuss a few current theoretical issues. I do so, not to correct or instruct practitioners, but to reassure. The experimental analysis of behavior is developing rapidly, and at every step the principles of behavior therapy gain authority. Troublesome behavior is caused by troublesome contingencies of reinforcement, not by troublesome feelings or states of mind, and we can correct the trouble by correcting the contingencies.

RESPONDENT BEHAVIOR THERAPY

Psychotherapy has often been concerned with feelings, with anxiety, fear, anger, and the like. An early step toward behavior therapy was the realization that what was felt was not a "feeling" but a state of the body. The point was made before the advent of behaviorism by William James and Carl Lange. Lange looked for possibly relevant states, but James put the argument in its best known form: we do not cry because we are sad, we are sad because we cry.

A further step was needed. We do not cry *because* we are sad or feel sad *because* we cry, we cry *and* feel sad because something has happened. Perhaps a friend has died. We must know something about the earlier event if we are to explain either the crying or the state felt. That is the behavioristic position: turn to antecedent environmental events to explain what one does and, at the same time, what one feels while doing it. For every state felt and given the name of a feeling there is presumably a prior environmental event of which it is the product. Behavior therapy addresses the prior event rather than the feeling.

What are felt as emotions are, of course, largely the responses of glands and smooth muscle. Efforts were once made to define a given emotion as a particular pattern of such responses. The variables of which the behavior is a function are a more promising alternative. Some of them are genetic; emotional behavior has evolved because of its contribution to the survival of the species. Variables of that sort are largely out of reach in dealing with the behavior of an individual, although instinctive emotional behavior can often be allowed to adapt out. Much more can be done when emotional responses result from respondent (Pavlovian) conditioning. Troublesome behavior can then often be extinguished, or other behavior can be conditioned to replace it. Both adaptation and extinction have fewer unwanted side effects when stimuli are presented with gradually increasing intensities. The process is called, of course, desensitization.

OPERANT BEHAVIOR THERAPY

Therapists have been as much concerned with what people do as with what they feel. Behavior therapists trace what is done to two kinds of selective consequences, innate behavior to natural selection and learned behavior to operant reinforcement. A given instance is usually a joint product of both. There is an operant side to emotion, for example. Fear is not only a response of glands and smooth muscle, it is a reduced probability of moving toward a feared object and a heightened probability of moving away from it. The operant side of anger is a greater probability of hurting someone and a lesser probability of pleasing. Where the bodily state resulting from respondent conditioning is usually called a feeling, the state resulting from operant conditioning, observed through introspection, is more often called a state of mind.

Important distinctions are obscured, however, when behavior is attributed to a state of mind. An operant is strengthened, for example, when a response has reinforcing consequences, but subsequent responses occur because of what has happened, not what is going to happen. When we say that we do something "with the intention of producing a given effect," we attribute our behavior to something that lies in the future, but both the behavior and the state introspectively observed at the time are due to what has happened in the past.

Expectation misrepresents the facts in the same way. To take an operant example, when a reinforcing consequence has followed something we have done, we are said to expect that it will follow when we do it again. What is introspectively observed is the bodily state resulting from the past occurrence. When one stimulus has often followed another, regardless of anything we may have done, we are said to *expect* the second whenever the first occurs. That *expectation* is a bodily state resulting from respondent conditioning.

Terms for states of mind have never been consistently used. The nervous systems which bring our behavior into contact with various parts of our own body are not very efficient because they evolved for other reasons, and we cannot observe many of the bodily states of other people at all, at least while they are alive. In any case, explanations of that sort must themselves be explained. We make no progress by explaining one state of mind as the effect of another; we must get back to something that can be directly observed and, if possible, put to use. That means, of course, the genetic and personal histories responsible both for the behavior and, in passing, the states of the body introspectively observed.

Some Examples

The operant side of behavior therapy can be illustrated by considering a few characteristic problems, in each of which behavior is traced to a contingency of natural selection or operant reinforcement rather than to a state of mind.

Positively reinforced behavior is often accompanied by a state which we report by saying that we are doing "what we want to do," "like to do," or "love to do." There is a special reason why such behavior is often troublesome. The reinforcing effect of a particular consequence may have evolved under conditions that no longer prevail. For example, most of us are strongly reinforced by salty or sweet foods, not because large quantities are good for us now, but because salty and sweet foods were in short supply in the early history of the species. Those for whom, thanks to genetic variations, these foods were especially reinforcing were more likely to eat them and survive. The increased susceptibility to reinforcement then led to the discovery and processing of vast quantities of salty and sweet foods; and many of us now eat too much of them and may turn to therapy for help.

An increased susceptibility to reinforcement by sexual contact would also have had great survival value in a world subject to famine, pestilence, and predation. However, it now raises problems, not only for individuals but for an already overpopulated world. A strong susceptibility to reinforcement by signs that one has hurt another person could also have evolved, because such signs shape and maintain skillful combat. (The boxer who shows that he has been hurt has taught his opponent how to hurt.) Hence, aggressive behavior has been strongly reinforced, which, like that of sexual behavior, raises problems both for the individual and the world as a whole.

Problems also arise from reinforcers which have never had any evolutionary advantage. *Homo sapiens* is not the only species to have discovered them. The reinforcing effects of alcohol, heroin, cocaine, and other drugs are presumably accidental. They are particularly troublesome when use leads to the powerful negative reinforcers we call withdrawal symptoms. The craving from which addicts suffer is a bodily state due to an anomalous reinforcer.

The Operant Side of Behavior Therapy

A different problem arises when a repertoire of behavior conditioned in one environment undergoes extinction in another. The relevant bodily state may be called discouragement, a sense of failure, helplessness, a loss of confidence, or depression. A different kind of depression follows when, having acquired a large and effective repertoire, one moves to a place in which it cannot be executed. The behavior itself is not extinguished (there are things one still wants to do); but appropriate occasions for expressing the behavior are lacking. The student who has acquired an effective repertoire in college finds no place for it in the world to which he moves upon graduation. The person who moves to a different city may suffer the same kind of depression when a repertoire appropriate to the old city does not work well in the new.

The addiction caused by anomalous reinforcers is quite different from the addiction caused by certain schedules of reinforcement. The so-called variable-ratio schedule is especially likely to cause trouble. It is a useful schedule because it maintains behavior against extinction when reinforcers occur only infrequently. For example, the behavior of a dedicated artist, writer, businessman, or scientist is sustained by occasional, unpredictable reinforcements. We play games because our behavior is reinforced on a variable ratio schedule, and for the same reason we gamble. In the long run gamblers lose because those who maintain the contingencies must win. As with the behavior caused by anomalous reinforcers, gambling is an addiction in the sense that there is no ultimate gain, at least for most of those who gamble.

Many problems that require therapy arise from a fault in operant conditioning itself. The process presumably evolved because behavior was strengthened when it had important consequences for both individual and species. The process could not, however, take into account the *manner* in which the behavior produced its consequences. It was enough that consequences followed, even though they were produced by many different things done. Conditioning occurs when reinforcing consequences follow for any reason whatsoever.

Accidental consequences yield the behavior we call superstition. We fall ill, take a pill or perform a ritual, and get well, and we are more likely to take a pill or perform the ritual when we fall ill again, regardless of whether there was any actual effect.[1] Superstitions may stand in the way of better measures. Therapy is often a matter of destroying the reinforcing effects of adventitious consequences.

---

[1] Feeling better is probably too long deferred a consequence to act as a reinforcer. Superstitions of that kind need verbal mediation. Recalling the two events brings them together in an effective way. The variable schedules in sports and games of chance produce mannerisms and "styles" which are better examples of the basic effect.

Aversive consequences are responsible for many kinds of problems. As negative reinforcers, they can have the faults we have just seen in positive reinforcers. As punishment, their side effects may be severe. We learned to crawl, walk, run, and ride a bicycle not only because getting around in the world reinforced our correctly doing so but also because we were hurt when we made mistakes. This sort of punishment is immediately contingent on behavior and may reduce its probability of occurrence, but it can also suppress behavior in a different way through respondent conditioning. The situation in which the behavior occurs or some aspect of the behavior itself becomes aversive, and it can then negatively reinforce alternative forms of behavior. A punished person remains as strongly inclined as ever to behave in the punished way but escapes from the threat of punishment by doing something else. When punishment is imposed by other people, as it often is, it is seldom immediately contingent on what is done and is more likely to work via respondent conditioning.

The bodily state resulting from the threat of punishment is named according to its source. When punished by one's peers it is called *shame*, when by a government *guilt*, and when by a religious agency a *sense of sin*. One way to escape is to confess and take the punishment, but when the behavior on which a deferred punishment was contingent is not always clear, escape can be difficult. Merely accidental aversive contingencies generate unexplained feelings of shame, guilt, or sin, and a person may then turn to a therapist for help in escaping.

Here, then, are a few examples of troublesome contingencies of operant reinforcement, together with a few "states of mind" to which the behavior is often attributed. Other examples could be given (the list seems endless), but these are perhaps enough to show the greater precision and potential of the operant analysis. It does not follow, however, that behavior therapists should never ask their clients what they are feeling or thinking. From their clients' answers something may be inferred about their genetic or personal histories. Asking such questions is, in fact, often the only way therapists can learn about a personal history. They lack the facilities needed for direct investigations, and to investigate without permission is unethical. But asking about feelings and thoughts is only a convenience—the very convenience, in fact, which explains why people have asked about them for so many centuries—and we must turn to more accessible variables if we are to promote a scientific analysis or use it to do something about personal problems.

The argument for operant behavior therapy is essentially this: What are felt as feelings or introspectively observed as states of mind are states of the body, and they are the products of certain contingencies of reinforcement. The contingencies can be much more easily identified and analyzed than feelings or states of mind, and by turning to them as the thing to be changed, behavior therapy gains a special advantage. An important question remains to be answered, however. How are contingencies to be changed?

Changing the Contingencies

The conditions of which behavior is a function are sometimes under control, in homes, for example, and in schools, workplaces, hospitals, and prisons. Therapists may change these conditions for their own purposes if they are part of a family or if they teach, employ workers, or administer hospitals or prisons. Professionally, they advise those who do so. They help parents with their children or spouses with their spouses; they advise teachers; they recommend new practices in hospitals and prisons. They can do so because some of the conditions under which people live can be controlled.

The word *control* raises a familiar issue. What right has a therapist to manipulate the conditions of which a person's behavior is a function? The question is more often asked about the use of punitive consequences by governments or positive reinforcers by business and industry. If it is not so often asked of psychotherapists, it is because they have not demonstrated any threatening power or because, like Carl Rogers, they insist that they are not exercising control at all. The question is more likely to be asked of behavior therapists because they are more often effective. Token economies in hospitals or prisons, for example, have been challenged precisely because they work. Food, even institutional food, is a reinforcer and can often be made contingent on behavior. That can be done to the advantage of those who are reinforced, but it is perhaps more often done to solve problems of management. The ethical question would seem to be *cui bono*, who profits? Control is ethical if it is exerted for the sake of the controlled.

That principle of control could play a greater part in current demands for legislative action to prohibit the use of aversive measures by therapists. It is easy to argue for banning the use of aversives because they are unpleasant things. By definition they are things we turn away from, and when used as punishment they interfere with things we want to do. But who eventually profits? The dentist's drill is aversive, but we accept it to escape a toothache. We accept the punitive practices of governments and religions in return for some measure of order, security, and peace of mind. When aversive stimuli are used to stop the bizarre behavior of autistic people long enough to bring them under the control of non-aversive practices, they would seem to be justified.

But aversive stimuli should be justified only if no other measure can be used. Too ready an acceptance of aversive measures blocks progress along better lines. Only recently have strong sanctions been imposed on child abuse by parents and the battering of spouses, and corporal punishment is only now being strongly challenged in schools. We are not yet ready to replace a police force or close the Pentagon. Applied behavior analysis has contributed to alternative measures, however, and we may hope that the problems of the autistic will soon be solved in better ways.

THE CLINIC

Homes, schools, workplaces, hospitals, and prisons are environments in which people spend a great deal of time. Face-to-face therapy in the clinic is different. Only a small part of the client's life is spent in the presence of a therapist. Only a few reinforcers can be used, and most of the time only to reinforce social, especially verbal, behavior. There is a great deal of mutual shaping of behavior in face-to-face confrontations.

What the client does in the clinic is not of primary concern, however. What happens there is preparation for a world which is not under the control of the therapist. Instead of arranging current contingencies of reinforcement, as in a home, school, workplace, or hospital, therapists give advice. Modeling behavior to be copied is a kind of advice, but verbal advice has a broader scope. It may take the form of an order ("Do this, stop doing that") or it may describe contingencies of reinforcement ("Doing this will probably have a reinforcing effect." "If you do that the consequences may be punishing.").

Traditionally, advice has been thought of as communication. Something called knowledge of the world is said to pass from speaker to listener. But a useful distinction has been made between knowing by acquaintance and knowing by description. Knowing because something you have done has had reinforcing consequences is very different from knowing because you have been told what to do; it is the difference between contingency-shaped and rule-governed behavior.

But why is advice taken? Children often do as they are told because they have been punished when they have not done so, and something of the sort is suggested in therapy when it is said that the therapist should become an authority figure, perhaps that of a father or mother. But children also do as they are told because positive reinforcers have followed. Parents who contrive positive consequences are said to "reward" their children for doing as they are told. Teachers contrive similar reinforcing consequences, such as commendation or good grades, to induce their students to study. There is no natural connection between the behavior and its consequences, but the practice is justified on the grounds that genuine consequences will take over in the world at large. Nothing of that sort is suitable in therapy. The reinforcing consequences available to induce clients to take advice are to be found outside the clinic.

Therapists who resemble people whose advice has often proved to be worth taking have an advantage. Those who do not must work in other ways. In traditional terms, they must build "confidence" or "trust." That can sometimes be done by giving bits of advice which are not only easily followed but will almost certainly have reinforcing consequences.

Face-to-face advice may also take the form of rules for effective action. The proverbs and maxims of cultures are rules of that sort. They are especially useful because therapists may not be available to help when new problems arise. Not every problem can be solved by applying a rule, however, and therapists may need to take a further step and teach their clients how to construct their own rules. That means teaching them something about the analysis of behavior—a task that is usually easier than teaching them how to change their feelings or states of mind.

HEALTH

Psychotherapy is said to promote mental health in the sense of helping people "feel well" and "think clearly." Behavior therapy promotes behavioral health in the sense that it helps people behave well, not in the sense of politely, but successfully. Is there an effect on physical health?

What people do may have obvious medical consequences—what they eat, how much they exercise, how carefully they avoid accidents, whether they smoke, drink, or take drugs, how often they expose themselves to infection, what medicines they take, or how well they follow medical advice. Operant therapists can improve medical health by helping people manage themselves in such ways. But is there a direct effect?

Something of the sort is suggested when it is said that a given type of personality or neurosis is associated with a given type of physical illness. If psychotherapists change personalities or neuroses, they should be able to change health. But personality explains nothing until we have explained personality, and as an internal correlate of behavior a neurosis is no more useful here than elsewhere. The *person* in personality once meant the mask worn by an actor in a Greek play. It defined him as a *persona dramatis*. The word *neurology* was invented in the early 19th century at about the same time as *phrenology*. Phrenologists claimed to locate traits of character in the gross structure of the skull. Neurology went further inside to the gross structure of the nervous system. The important facts, then as now, were what people did. Behavior therapists turn to the contingencies of reinforcement responsible for the behavior that personality, neuroses, and the like are said to explain.

To say that physical illness is due to *stress*, for example, does not explain the illness or point to any way to treat it until stress has been explained. If people are under stress because, for example, there are too many things they must do, the number of things they must do should change. To do anything about illness due to *anxiety* we must change the aversive circumstances responsible for what is thus felt. Some of the illness said to be due to *discouragement* or *despair* may be alleviated by restoring lost reinforcers, and illness due to *hostility* or *fear* by eliminating aversive consequences, especially at the hands of other people. Assertions of this sort do not ignore genetic factors. Behavior therapy is limited to changes that can be made during a person's lifetime.

A very different relation between behavior and health is implied when it is said that a critically ill patient simply "refuses to die" or that one with a favorable prognosis loses the "will to live." Examples of that sort are, of course, said to show the power of mind over matter. They suggest that being healthy is something one *does*. Ancient metaphors of the medical profession may be responsible. We "catch" a cold or "get" the measles. Engaged in a war with disease, we are attacked (we have a "heart attack") or struck down (we have a "stroke"). When infections invade us, much depends on our "resistance." But good health is not contingent on behavior in such a way as to reinforce "being healthy" as a kind of action.

How contingencies of operant reinforcement affect physiological processes is no doubt an important question. Can immunological reactions be conditioned in the Pavlovian manner, for example? But should the behavior therapist try to find out? Physiology has a special appeal to those who explain behavior in mentalistic terms because it seems to show what is *really* going on inside, what one is *really* talking about. Cognitive psychologists have turned to brain science for that reason. Behavior therapists may also turn to physiology if they lack confidence in their own methods, but those methods are quite as objective. One cannot quarrel with the choice of medical science as a professional field, or even with philosophers who wish to examine their minds through introspection, but for every behavior therapist who, upon discovering some fact about behavior, then looks for a physiological explanation, there is one fewer therapist to make further studies of behavior itself.

The Operant Side of Behavior Therapy

FEELING WELL AND FEELING GOOD

People usually seek both medical and behavior therapy because of how they feel. The physician changes what they feel in medical ways; behavior therapists change the contingencies of which feelings are a function. The distinction between medical and behavior therapy resembles the distinction between feeling well and feeling good. One feels well who feels a healthy body, free of aches or pains. One feels good who feels a body which has been positively reinforced. Positive reinforcers please. We call them pleasant and the behavior they reinforce a pleasure. They please even when they are accidental. (*Happy* first meant "lucky.")

What is felt in that way is apparently a strong probability of action and a freedom from aversive stimuli. We are "eager" to do things which have had reinforcing consequences and "feel better" in a world in which we do not "have" to do unpleasant things. We say that we are enjoying life or that life is good. We have no complaints because complaining is a kind of negatively reinforced behavior, and there are no negative reinforcers. Successful therapy builds strong behavior by removing unnecessary negative reinforcers and multiplying positive ones. Whether or not those whose behavior is thus strengthened live any longer than other people, they can at least be said to live well.

Finding a world in which one can live well in spite of infirmities is the theme of *Enjoy Old Age* (1983), a little book written with the collaboration of Margaret Vaughan. Certain medical imperfections in old age cannot be avoided. Aversive consequences are more likely to follow whatever one does and reinforcing consequences less often. But the *world* of old people can often be changed so that, in spite of imperfections, one can enjoy more of one's life and perhaps even live a little longer.

Can something of the sort be done for everyone? My utopian novel, *Walden Two* (1948), published forty years ago, was a fictional anticipation of what came to be called applied behavior analysis. It describes a community in which governmental, religious, and capitalistic agencies are replaced by face-to-face personal control. New members begin by following simple rules, with the help of instruction and counseling, and their behavior is soon taken over by carefully designed social contingencies. Both operant and respondent conditioning are used. Children learn to manage their emotions, for example, through desensitization. There is little or no negative reinforcement or punishment. (Curiously enough, many critics complained that the citizens of *Walden Two* were too happy.) Like all utopias, *Walden Two* tries to solve the problems of a culture all at once rather than one by one. We shall probably not move rapidly toward that kind of better world, but it is, I think, worth considering as a model. Every advance in behavior therapy moves in that direction because it begins by changing the world in which people live and then, only indirectly, what they do and feel.

For thousands of years philosophers have talked about the behavior of people with whom they have had no contact and about whose feelings or states of mind they could not ask. Instead they have disembodied mental events and discussed them quite apart from anyone in whom they occur. They have said that frustration breeds aggression, that greed overrides caution, that jealousy destroys affection. Statements of this sort are fairly common in current discussions of government, religion, economics, and the other so-called (but in this case miscalled) behavioral sciences. By rejecting feelings and states of mind as the initiating causes of behavior, and turning instead to the environmental conditions responsible both for what people do and feel while doing it, behavior analysts, and with them behavior therapists, can approach the larger problems of human behavior in a much more effective way.

A problem of far greater importance remains to be solved. Rather than build a world in which we shall all live well, we must stop building one in which it will be impossible to live at all. This issue is wholly a problem of human behavior. How are people to be induced to consume no more than they need, refrain from unnecessarily polluting the environment, have only enough children to replace themselves, and solve international problems without risking a nuclear war? The contingencies under which people now live are maintained by governments, religions, and economic enterprises, but those institutions are in turn controlled by fairly immediate consequences which are increasingly incompatible with the future of the world. We need to construct relatively immediate consequences of human behavior which will act as the remoter consequences would act if they were here now. That will not be easy, but at least we can say that we have a science and a technology that address the basic problem.

◆ CHAPTER 8 ◆

The School of the Future

Ａs I have said before," "As we have seen," "To repeat,"—these are all expressions of the sort I have called autoclitics (1957).We use them to tell the listener or reader something about what we are on the point of saying—in these examples, that it will be something we have said before. We say things more than once for many reasons. Perhaps we have not been understood; perhaps the listener or reader has forgotten and must be reminded. Another reason is not always acknowledged. Jorge Luis Borges, the Argentinian poet, was frank about it: "What can I do at 71," he said, "but plagiarize myself?" It is not necessarily a fault of age. When one has acquired a large verbal repertoire, one has a great many things to say, and too often they simply pop out. During the past 30 years, for example, I have published 25 papers or chapters in books on education. What are the chances that I shall now say something that I have not said before?

I claim the right to repeat. Whether or not what I have said has been understood or remembered, it certainly has not had much of an effect on American schools. They are no better (they are probably worse) than when I began to talk about them. Nevertheless, to protect you as far as possible from self-plagiarism, I have not reread any of those 25 papers while preparing this one—with one exception: A paper called "Programmed Instruction Revisited" (1986), from which the following chapter was excerpted. It was written only a year or two ago and, perhaps for that reason, its first paragraph still seems to me just right, and I cannot resist quoting it:

> The public school was invented to bring the services of a private tutor to more than one student at a time. As the number of students increased, each one necessarily received less attention. By the time

the number had reached 25 or 30, personal attention could be sporadic at best. Textbooks were invented to take over some of the work of the tutor, but they could not do two important things. They could not, as the tutor did, immediately evaluate what each student said, nor could they tell the student exactly what to do next. Teaching machines and programmed texts were invented to restore those important features of tutorial instruction.

As that paragraph implies, the history of education has been the history of small adjustments in an established system. The trouble with American education is clearly one of size. The larger the school or class the worse the problem faced by the teacher. Growth, however, has been so slow that educators have missed the crucial fault. Something is wrong with the situation in which teaching occurs. Like gamblers who eventually lose their fortunes, educators have played a game that has grown less and less profitable. Gamblers continue to play because they sometimes win, and we go on with the same system in education because teachers sometimes teach well. Some people are good teachers; they would be good at almost anything they did. They can hold the attention, and even the affection, of large numbers of students. Some young people are good students. They scarcely need to be taught. They learn in spite of the quality of teacher or school. American education turns out some successful products. But not enough of them. Not enough teachers can teach well under present conditions, and not enough students can learn when badly taught. We need schools in which available teachers will successfully teach students of a wide range of abilities.

GOING TO SCHOOL AND STUDYING

The word *school* comes from the Greek by way of the Latin. Surprising as it may seem to most teachers and students, it first meant "rest" or "leisure." Then it meant what one did when at leisure, and that was talk. Then it meant a *place* in which to talk and, when the talk became formal, a place for lectures and disputation. It still means primarily a place to talk. Even when students do other things—paint pictures, play music, dance, do scientific experiments—talk is essential. A school of art differs from an artist's studio because what is painted in the school is talked about.

But what does talking mean? In the older view, now revived by cognitive psychologists, it meant imparting knowledge. *Cognition* means knowledge, but cognitive psychologists prefer the word *information*. Listeners are said to "extract information from what speakers say and process and store it for future use." Perhaps cognitive psychologists prefer *information* because it seems more objective and, indeed, the storage and retrieval of information are real enough in other settings. The alphabet seems to have come into use to keep records when goods were exchanged between buyers and sellers. The records were stored and, when accounts were settled, retrieved. That was better than remembering what had been exchanged. But does anything like that happen when people learn from each other?

An extraordinary step in the evolution of the human species brought its vocal musculature under operant control. The social environments we call languages then evolved. With their help, a person could profit from what another person had learned and, with the help of the alphabet, from what many other people had learned. Until that time the species had learned as other species still do, under contingencies of reinforcement. With the evolution of language, they learned from descriptions of contingencies.

Consider a simple example. Occasionally a door can be opened only by sliding it to one side. Perhaps we discover this by sliding it when it has not opened in other ways. A cognitive psychologist would say that we then "know how to open the door." Then we see a friend pushing and pulling the door and we say, "Slide it to one side." In doing so we specify an action and imply a reinforcing consequence. Or we say, "The door opens when you slide it to one side," describing the contingencies more fully. A cognitive psychologist would say that our friend also then knows how to open the door or how the door can be opened. But there is a great difference. Our knowledge was what Bertrand Russell called "knowledge by acquaintance," but our friend's is as yet only "knowledge by description." When she then pushes the door to one side and opens it, however, her knowledge changes from one kind to the other. As a behavior analyst would put it, her behavior is first rule-governed and then becomes contingency-shaped.

Something of the sort is what happens in education. Students almost always begin with knowledge by description. They are told what can be done or what will happen when something is done. If what they learn is worthwhile, they will eventually acquire knowledge by acquaintance when their behavior has reinforcing consequences. But that usually happens much later. Schools prepare students for a world which lies rather far in the future.

There are great differences between rule-governed and contingency-shaped behavior. Behavior said to be due to knowledge by acquaintance (the product of immediate contingencies of reinforcement) is much more effectively executed than knowledge by description. Try teaching your friend how to swim by telling her what she is to do with her head, arms, and legs or why she will then move smoothly through the water. The behavior also differs in what is usually called motivation. Our friend first opened the door as she was told to do because reinforcing consequences had followed when we or others like us had given her other advice. The consequences were probably not contingent on the kind of behavior executed in this instance. The opened door, following immediately, has a greater strengthening effect. Educators have tried to promote knowledge by acquaintance—for example, by "bringing real life into the classroom," by teaching botany with a few plants and zoology with a vivarium and aquarium, but little of the world for which 12 years of school prepares a student can be made available during those 12 years. Rule-governed behavior must wait a long time before becoming contingency-shaped. That is why schools must remain places where students listen and read.

But why do they pay attention to their teachers and read their books? The traditional answer is not often acknowledged: in one way or another they have been punished when they have failed to do so. The birch rod, the cane, the paddle—those were once the tools of the teacher, and until recently they were often viciously used. There is biblical authority: "Who spares the rod, hateth his son." (Daughters were not taught, of course.) Oliver Goldsmith's Irish schoolmaster never "spoils the child and spares the rod/But spoils the rod and never spares the child."

Punishment, a standard way to *suppress* behavior, is almost the only way other animals control each other, and we have retained much of that practice. Governments use punishment to suppress the troublesome behavior of citizens and other governments. But punishing for "not studying" is different. The aim is to strengthen behavior, not to suppress it. The aversive stimuli are used as negative reinforcers. The same unwanted by-products follow, however. Students escape if they can, playing hookey or dropping out, and counterattack by vandalizing schools and assaulting teachers.

Less conspicuous forms of punishments are still troublesome. I often ask college students about their "motivation": "When you go to your room tonight, is it not true that you will be studying primarily to avoid the consequences of not doing so?" They seldom say no. The subtle by-products of negative reinforcement are then harder to spot.

So-called token economies were introduced into education to avoid the harmful by-products of punishment. A 6th-grade teacher once told me how she had solved a problem. Her students had not been doing their homework or finishing their classroom assignments. They paid little attention to threats of punishment, in part because she could not really back them up. On the point of "burning out," she turned to positive reinforcement. One Monday morning she brought a small pocket radio to school and told her students that one of them would win it in a lottery at the end of the week. For each completed homework or classroom assignment, a student could write his or her name on a card and put it in a jar. On Friday afternoon a winning name would be drawn. The more cards, of course, the better the student's chances. The next week she brought in another prize and held another lottery. By the end of the second week, she said, her problem was solved. Her students almost always brought in their homework and finished their assignments. At the cost of a few dollars a week she began to live a much more comfortable life, and she also had the satisfaction of knowing that she was teaching well, at least to the extent that the homework and classroom assignments she was required to use taught well.

Token economies are usually ridiculed by educators. One should not get an education by getting prizes. Education should be its own prize. Prizes are said to mask or even destroy the effect of the real consequences. But that is also true of punishment. The fact is that neither rewards nor punishments have anything to do with teaching if they merely keep students in contact with teachers and books. They cannot teach, because they are not properly contingent on the behavior we take to show the possession of knowledge.

TEACHING

Members of other species "acquire knowledge" from each other through imitation, a process traceable both to natural selection and operant conditioning. They sometimes model behavior to be imitated, but only members of the human species seem to do so because others then imitate them. Modeling is a kind of teaching, but it has a lasting effect only when supported by positive or negative reinforcement.

Let us say that you are in Japan and have gone to a master of origami to learn how to fold something. He does not speak English nor you Japanese, but he can *show* you how to fold. He will also need some way of saying "Right" and "Wrong." Someone has told him that you are an operant conditioner, and he shows you what you are going to make: a paper pigeon. He gives you a square sheet of paper and takes one himself. He makes a first fold with his sheet and waits for you to do the same. Only when you have done so, does he make another fold. That is his way of saying "Right." When your fold is wrong, he simply waits; waiting is saying "Wrong." When you try again and are right, he makes another fold. You continue in this way until you have made a paper

Professional Issues

pigeon, with beak, breast, wings, and tail, and when you pull its tail, its wings flap.

Of course you cannot yet fold one on your own. If it had been something very simple (a paper airplane, for example) you might have been able to do so, but learning a complex form calls for something more. The master gives you a fresh sheet of paper and takes one himself. This time he looks at you and waits. You are to make the first fold. When you do so, he does the same. He is saying "Right." You make another fold, and again he follows, but after another he simply waits. He is saying "Wrong." You try another fold, and he still waits. Eventually you stop. You cannot make the next fold. Perhaps he now makes it for you, but he will teach you most rapidly if he makes only part of it, just enough to enable you to go on. Eventually you complete a second pigeon. You still cannot make one without help, but as you make others, you will need less and less help and eventually none at all. The master has finished his assignment. You know how to make an origami pigeon.

What has happened? In modeling behavior to be imitated the master has *primed* your behavior in the sense of getting it to occur for the first time. Your behavior was first entirely imitative, but you took each step after taking another. The other steps slowly replaced the model as a discriminative stimulus, and they did so more rapidly as less behavior was modeled. That is why the master showed you only part of a step you had forgotten. Instead of priming the step, he prompted it. (The prompter in the theater gives the actor only part of the forgotten line. Giving it all would be telling.) Borrowing a word from the magician, we say that the master "vanished" primes and prompts by removing them as rapidly as possible.

Verbal behavior can be taught in the same way. As I have said before (remember Borges!), I taught my younger daughter to recite 15 lines of Longfellow's *Evangeline* quickly and painlessly by priming, prompting, and vanishing the prompts. I wrote the lines on a blackboard and asked her to read them. The lines primed her behavior. Then I erased a few words essentially at random and asked her to "read" the lines. She could do so because the words which remained on the board were effective prompts. I removed other words and asked her to read the lines again. Within a few minutes she was "reading" them although nothing was on the blackboard. (When I recently told her that I was going to use this story in this chapter, she immediately ran off the first two lines: "Up the staircase moved a luminous space in the darkness/ Lighted less by the lamp than the shining face of the maiden." She had learned them more than a quarter of a century earlier.)

We go through the same steps when we memorize a poem by ourselves. We prime our behavior by reading the poem, and we say as much of it as we can without help, glancing at the text for primes or prompts but only as needed. Eventually we recite the poem.

When we learn to make an origami pigeon or memorize a poem, we acquire behavior of a given topography of behavior. The stimuli which take control are generated by the behavior itself. That may seem like an inferior kind of knowledge, but verbal behavior is brought under the control of other kinds of stimuli in the same way. We teach a very young child to speak a word by priming it. We say "Dada" or "Mama" and reinforce any reasonable approximation. We bring a verbal response under the control of an object by showing the object, speaking the word, and reinforcing a fair approximation. We hold up a spoon, say "Spoon," and reinforce any reasonable response. Later we wait for a response to be made to the spoon alone. We teach what a word means by speaking the word and holding up an object. Later, we reinforce pointing to the object when we have spoken the word. Children do not need such explicit instruction, of course. They learn to talk, but much more slowly, under the contingencies of reinforcement maintained by a verbal environment.

CONTINGENCIES OF REINFORCEMENT

An opened door, progress in making a paper pigeon, reciting a few lines of poetry without help, or expressions of delight by parents—these are immediate reinforcing consequences and in that respect are very different from rewards or punishments in the classroom. Unfortunately it is not easy to arrange similar consequences for what students must do. A very powerful reinforcer is available, however. It does not need to be contrived for instructional purposes; it is unrelated to any particular kind of behavior and hence always available. We call it success.

Throughout the history of the species and the personal history of the individual, successful manipulation of the environment has preceded the consequences which have played their part in natural selection and operant conditioning. Successful manipulation reinforces whatever we do in achieving a specific consequence. It reinforces opening a door no matter where we are going. We are more aware of its importance when it is missing (when the door sticks). Successful manipulation of the environment is a weak reinforcer, but it can have a powerful effect if it occurs often enough. The trouble with present classroom practices is that students seldom do anything which is immediately or visibly successful.

Professional Issues

TEACHING MACHINES

Teaching machines were designed to take advantage of the reinforcing power of immediate consequences. More than 60 years ago Sidney Pressey invented a machine which administered a multiple-choice test. Students pushed buttons to select their answers and, as Pressey pointed out, because they were told immediately whether they were right or wrong, the machine not only tested but taught; Pressey (1932) foresaw the coming "industrial revolution" in education. In 1954, at the University of Pittsburgh, I demonstrated a different teaching machine, which was a mechanical anticipation of the computer. (A better model, made by IBM, is now in the Smithsonian.) It presented a problem in arithmetic, which the student solved by moving figures into place. The machine sensed the solution and, if it was correct, led the student on to the next problem.

The two machines differed in three important ways. (a) Pressey's was to be used after the student had already studied a subject. It supplied a kind of confirmation of right answers. Mine taught from the beginning. (b) With Pressey's machine, students selected their responses; with mine, they composed them. That is a great difference. It is possible to read another language fluently, for example, and get a perfect grade on a multiple-choice test without being able to speak it. (c) The material in Pressey's machine was not programmed. (It could have been, and programs were later written for similar machines.) My machine was designed to profit from what we had learned about the immediacy of reinforcement in the experimental analysis of behavior. Students took very small steps, and to make sure that they did so successfully, their behavior was carefully primed or prompted and then reinforced. Primes and prompts were "vanished" as fast as possible.

I was soon using a machine based on the same principles to teach part of a course in human behavior, with a program written in collaboration with James G. Holland (1961). *As I have said many times,* Allan Calvin used rather similar machines in a school in Roanoke, Virginia, to teach an 8th-grade class *all* of 9th-grade algebra in half a year. The class scored above the 9th-grade norms when tested a year later.

For a few years a teaching machine movement flourished. Hundreds of articles and scores of books were published about it. Catalogs of available programs began to be published annually.[1] A quarter of a

---

[1] By the end of 1962, according to an editorial in *Science*, 250 programmed courses would be available in elementary, secondary, and college mathematics; 60 in science; 25 in electronics and engineering; 25 in foreign languages; and 120 in social studies. Many were excellent. A colleague once told me that he had decided that he ought to know more about biochemistry, so he had bought a programmed text. "It was amazing!" he said. "In a week I knew biochemistry!" He did not mean that he was then a biochemist, of course, but he had learned a great deal in a remarkably short period of time with very little effort.

century later, however, programmed instruction in schools is rare. It failed to find a place in schools, but it is alive and well in industry, where millions of dollars worth of instructional programs are sold every year. Teaching in industry was once called training, and more or less dismissed as such, but what managers and employees now need to learn is similar to what is taught in schools and colleges. Teaching machines are missing from schools not because programmed instruction failed but because no one in the educational system is held accountable if a better way to teach is overlooked.

While my colleagues and I were learning how to write instructional programs, the Soviet Union was preparing to send a satellite around the world. Sputnik shocked America. Why had we not done it first? Our schools must be at fault. The National Defense Education Act was quickly passed, and large sums of money were made available for the improvement of teaching, especially in mathematics and science. A committee of experts met at Wood's Hole, Massachusetts, to plan the future.

Cognitive psychology was only beginning to be talked about at that time, but it seemed to be just the right thing. It was heralded as a return to the traditional study of the mind, and those who embarked on the improvement of our schools had never left that tradition. Education was held to be too important to be left to educators; mathematicians and scientists themselves would prepare the new materials.

Teachers were soon being told how mathematicians really thought, and they were to learn and teach students to think that way too. That was the New Math. Physics was also affected. A good example was the work of Jerrold Zacharias at MIT. Zacharias was a distinguished physicist and a great teacher, whose work was lavishly supported. One of his colleagues told me that America would no longer need a windfall of great physicists like those who had come from abroad in the 1930s for political reasons. It was not long, however, before the truth was out. Our schools were not producing better mathematicians or physicists than before Sputnik. Zacharias blamed the teachers, but what was wrong was that the new materials were being taught in the same old way.

Thirty years later, although cognitive psychologists still control schools of education, students are not processing, storing, or retrieving information any more successfully than before. Nor have other promises been kept. Cognitive psychologists reassure themselves by attacking behavioristic practices, but they have supplied little to put in their place. It is said, for example, that measures based on the study of nonhuman animals necessarily overlook what is essentially human. But we shall never know what is essentially human until we have seen what animals can do. Teaching and learning are said to be forms of social behavior, whereas teaching machines are asocial or solitary. But the environment teaches without the help of teachers, and if it does not do so in schools it is only because comparable contingencies have been lacking.

Cognitive psychologists also see no chance for students to be creative when learning from programmed instruction. Like pre-Darwinians they believe in a creative mind. But the origin of behavior, like the origin of species, is to be found in variation and selection.

The computer is the ideal teaching machine. It still tends to be used, however, as a substitute for a lecturer and to teach as teachers of large classes do. Its real value lies elsewhere. It can bring "real life" into the classroom, at least in schematic form. That is one way it is used in industry. Employees cannot be taught to act appropriately during a meltdown in a nuclear power plant by creating real meltdowns, but meltdowns can be simulated on computers. Computers can teach best, however, by leading the student through carefully prepared instructional programs. They can prime and prompt behavior and reinforce it imme-diately. In addition computers can move the student on to the next appropriate step. Those are the essentials of good teaching. They are what a tutor with one or two students could do and what teachers with large classes simply cannot do.

THE SCHOOL OF THE FUTURE

It is hard to say what the school of the future will look like. Architecture will probably follow function, and the function of a school as a whole is not yet clear. We can be sure, however, that schools will be very different from anything we have yet seen. They will be pleasant places. Like well-managed stores, restaurants, and theatres, they will look good, sound good, smell good. Students will come to school, not because they are punished if they stay away, but because they are attracted by the school.

Students will spend more time in school. They will start younger, in part because less care will be available at home as mothers move into professions. Students will stay in school longer, in fact if not in principle, because there will be fewer dropouts. Schools will teach many more things. They will have to do so if they teach twice as much in the same time. If what is now taught in 12 years were taught in 6, instruction would be out of phase with personal growth, and businesses would have to find jobs for very young workers. Instead of finishing earlier, students will study many other things.

Programmed instruction will permit students to choose among many more fields because curricula will not be restricted to the compe-tence of available teachers. Bright students will be able to pursue given fields much further than is now possible because the programs will be available. Students will be free to move on to subjects that are particularly interesting and reinforcing in their own right. They will have fewer reasons to turn elsewhere for their reinforcers—for example, to sex, violence, and drugs.

Teachers will have more time to talk with their students. Classroom discussions are now rare and not very much like conversations among friends or colleagues. Few of us enjoy a conversation in which we are being evaluated. Among friends a bright response is applauded; in the classroom it is more likely to be punished as an effort to curry favor, and the punishments wielded by other students can be severe. In early Jesuit schools one student was explicitly pitted against an aemulus, someone to be emulated. When a student failed to answer, the teacher turned to the aemulus. They usually hated each other. Something of the sort has survived. In many classrooms it is said that good students do not answer quickly or at all or that they invent an occasional wrong answer to maintain an acceptable place in the group.

Teachers of the future will function more as counselors, probably staying in contact with given students for more than one year and getting to know them better. Teachers will be better able to help students choose fields that are likely to interest them. Rather than teach individuals ineffectively under current conditions, they will have the satisfaction of being part of a system that teaches all students well. In return for increased productivity, teaching will be not only a satisfying profession but a richly rewarded one.

Can we afford this kind of school? The real question is whether we can afford to continue with what we have now. In the long run good schools will save a great deal of money. Governments will not need to spend what they now spend because our schools are so bad. There will be less need for the police force, which now spends a good deal of time correcting for the failure of education. Governments will be better when the citizens who put them in power are wiser and more responsible. Business and industry, the ultimate supporters of education, will have a much more skilled labor force. Life will be better for everyone, and well-informed people will take a greater responsibility for the future of the world.

Am I giving you a utopian dream, an educational *Walden Two?* In one sense, yes. But utopias do come true. The institution called Solomon's House in Francis Bacon's *New Atlantis* brought science into government, and it became the model for the Royal Society. Edward Bellamy's *Looking Backward* made a strong impression on social thinking in America at the end of the 19th century. Communities patterned after *Walden Two* are by no means as impressive. There are only a few of them and they are small.

But the "behavioral engineering" that figured so prominently in *Walden Two* has clearly come true in the field of applied behavior analysis.

In another sense, however, the school of the future is no dream. *As I have said so many times, (and will now say for the last time), we can teach twice as much as is now taught in the classroom in the same time and with the same effort.* There are several hundred learning centers in American schools at the present time, in the design of which I played some part. They are used primarily to teach those who have trouble learning basic skills in existing classrooms. Students come to the centers and work by themselves. Each day they start where they left off the day before. They take steps in a carefully programmed sequence and, of course, receive an immediate report on what they have done. On the average, they cover more than a year and a half of reading each year—at least twice as much as they were doing in a regular classroom.

Start with that and all the rest follows as the night the day. *We know how to build better schools.* What is needed is to convince those who are now responsible for our schools that the structure of our present schools makes good teaching almost impossible. The views of governments, schools of education, school boards, administrators, teachers, and parents must change. Changing our schools will be troublesome and for a time costly. In the long run better schools will save billions of dollars and make the future of the world much brighter.

◆ CHAPTER 9 ◆

Programmed Instruction Revisited: Excerpts from Another Paper on Teaching Machines

The cognitive movement that followed Sputnik seemed to legitimize traditional theories of teaching and learning. Many educators were content with books such as *Talks to Teachers* (1899) by William James, which was written in the language of the layperson. Programmed instruction, by contrast, took advantage of what had been discovered about teaching and learning in a special discipline called the experimental analysis of behavior. My first programs were written when I was finishing an application of that analysis to verbal behavior (Skinner, 1957). By carefully constructing certain "contingencies of reinforcement," it is possible to change behavior quickly and to maintain it in strength for long periods of time. I can illustrate the central process, operant conditioning, with a story. Many years ago I published an article "How to Teach Animals" (1951). The editors of *Look* found it hard to believe and challenged me. If I could teach an animal as swiftly as I said I could, they wanted pictures. I accepted the challenge. I would teach a dog to stand on its hind legs in a matter of minutes. I would not touch the dog or attract its attention in any way. I would not give it any reason to stand up (as by holding a piece of meat above its head). I would simply reinforce its behavior.

Some preparation would be needed. A reinforcer is most powerful when it follows very quickly—optimally, within a fraction of a second. Giving a hungry dog a bit of meat is too slow. The dog has to see the meat and come and get it, and that takes time. If reinforcement is to be essentially instantaneous, a conditioned reinforcer is needed. In my article, I had explained how to condition the sound of a clicker as a reinforcer. Since we were going to take pictures, I would use the camera flash instead. The *Look* staff members were to buy a dog and give it its

97

daily ration in the following way: when the dog was moving about the room, they were to flash the light and then give the dog a bit of meat. It would soon respond to the flash by coming to be fed—and when, after a day or two, it did so instantly, I would take over.

When I saw the dog for the first time, I took the switch that operated the flash and told the photographer to keep his camera on the dog. I had put some horizontal lines on one wall of the room, and when the dog went near them, I flashed the light. The dog came to the *Look* reporter to be fed and then went back near the lines—predictably, because I had just reinforced its going there. Sighting across the dog's head, I chose a line somewhat above its normal position and reinforced the first movement that brought the head to that height. When the dog returned from being fed, an effect was clear: it was holding its head noticeably higher, and I could then choose a higher line. As I moved upward from line to line, the dog's forefeet began to come off the floor, and it was soon standing straight up, Q.E.D. Since there was some meat left, I continued this "differential reinforcement" until the dog was *leaping straight up*, its hindfeet nearly a foot off the floor. A picture had been taken with each flash, and *Look* published one showing the final spectacular leap.

You will not find a correct account of the kind of experiment I did with the dog in most introductory psychology textbooks. Some of them would say that I rewarded the dog for jumping. As the etymology shows, however, a reward is compensation or remuneration for services performed and is seldom immediately contingent on behavior. We reward people; we *reinforce* behavior. Other texts would say that the dog learned by trial and error. But the dog was not *trying* to do anything when it lifted its head, and it certainly did not learn anything from errors. Some texts would call lifting the head or standing up purposive or goal-directed behavior, but a goal has no effect on the behavior through which it is reached. Only past consequences have any effect.

Many educators would say that what I did with the dog was training, not teaching. If so, it was very much improved training. Dogs have been trained for centuries, and there are useful rules of thumb, but it is highly unlikely that even the most expert animal trainer could have brought about that much change in behavior in such a short time by conventional means. Teaching is more than training, but it uses the same behavioral processes.

Of course, we seldom teach in just that way. We do not teach a child to tie a knot by conditioning a reinforcer, giving the child two pieces of string, and then reinforcing any move that contributes to the fashioning of a knot. Instead, we *show* the child how to tie a knot; we model the behavior, and the child imitates us. But why should the child do so?

Programmed Instruction Revisited

Before we can show the child how to tie a knot, he or she must have learned to imitate, and that learning will have taken place through operant conditioning. Because the vocal musculature of the human species has come under operant control, we can also *tell* the child how to tie a knot, and in that case the need for an acquired operant repertoire is even more obvious.

Showing and telling are ways of "priming" behavior, of getting people to behave in a given way for the first time so that the behavior can be reinforced. We do not learn by imitating, however, or because we are told what to do. Consequences must follow. Consider how most of us learned to drive a car. At first, we turned the starting switch when we saw our instructor do so, we pressed the brake pedal when he or she said "press," and so on. But the moves we made had consequences. When we turned the switch, the engine started; when we pressed the brake pedal, the car slowed or stopped. Those were natural consequences, and they were more closely contingent on our behavior than were those flashes on the behavior of the dog. They eventually shaped skillful driving. As long as we were responding to instruction, the car moved but we were not driving it. We learned "how to drive," in the sense of driving well, only when the contingencies of reinforcement maintained by the car took over. We do not learn by doing, as Aristotle maintained; we learn when what we do has reinforcing consequences. To teach is to arrange such consequences.

The same two stages occur in learning to talk about things. Someone primes our behavior either by saying something that we repeat or by writing something that we read. When reinforcing consequences follow, we learn. For a time, our behavior may need to be "prompted." As it gains in strength, however, the prompts can be withdrawn or "vanished," in the sense in which a magician "vanishes" a bouquet of flowers.

It is often said that education is preparation. "Preparation for life" was once the phrase. Teachers often forget, however, that preparing is not the same as living. The consequences that induce students to come to school, listen to their teachers, watch demonstrations, study, and answer questions are not the consequences that will follow when they use what they have learned. Students and teachers tend to move too quickly to the "living" stage. The student who wishes to be a violinist or a tennis player usually wants to play too soon; students who demand the right to choose what they will study are usually trying to skip the instructional stage. Those who criticize programmed instruction by saying that students should learn to read *real* books also want to move out of the preparation stage too quickly.

Programmed instruction was designed to correct a basic fault: only rarely can behavior in a classroom be immediately reinforced, and a student cannot move on at once to new material. Hence teachers must resort to some kind of punishment. Such a return to aversive contingencies may be very subtle. One committee, studying schools, complained, typically, that "an alarming number of students leave high school with the idea that the adult world tolerates tardiness, absences, and misbehavior" and called for "stringent education standards and tough discipline." *Discipline* has come a long way from its original association with *disciple;* it now means "punishment," which, in turn, means more dropouts and more vandalism. The committee seemed to be aware of that and added that it wanted to "encourage maximum creativity on how these standards are achieved." In other words, the committee did not know how to achieve them. To return to punitive control is to admit that we have failed to solve a central problem in education. Correct responses and signs of progress are the kinds of reinforcers most appropriate to instruction as preparation, but other reinforcers must follow if there is any point in teaching.

People are said to write articles or books for money or acclaim. Those may be rewards, but they do not occur soon enough to be reinforcers. At one's desk the reinforcers are the appearances of sentences that make sense, clear up puzzles, answer questions, make points. Instructional programs in which students complete sentences, rather than select them from a set of multiple choices, have the same effect. Someone once said that programs that have blanks to be filled are like Swiss cheese, full of holes, but when students fill the holes with the right words, something happens that is very much like what happens when they use what they have learned. When we are writing a difficult paper and just the right word comes, a hole is filled and our behavior is reinforced.

It is sometimes said that programmed instruction gives too much help, that it does not "challenge" the student. But no amount of help is too much in the preparation stage. It must vanish, of course, as other reinforcers take over. The more helpful the program, the more (and more easily) the student learns. Some 350 years ago Comenius said, "The more the teacher teaches the *less* the student learns," but that is true only if it means "the less the student learns about learning." Some students profit from bad teaching because they learn how to teach themselves, but good teachers certainly have their place. How to study is a separate skill, and it can be taught, possibly by a program designed to do so.

The preparation stage of teaching raises a standard problem. Teachers cannot teach unless students pay attention. Students who "want an education" may pay attention for unidentified reasons, but what can be done with the others? Physical restraint is one solution, albeit a crude one. A teacher in a small private school once boasted that, to keep her students from looking out the window, she simply held her classes in a room without windows. In essence, she put blinders on her students. In the heyday of the teaching machine movement, a machine was advertised that held the student's head between earphones, confronting a brightly lighted page. The machine forced students to hear and see. Unfortunately, it did not teach them how to listen or look.

The threat of punishment falls short of physical restraint. Few words are spoken by teachers more often than, "Pay attention!" And these words are usually spoken with all the authority of *"Achtung!"* or "Now hear this!" Teachers who have relinquished the power to punish must resort to a pathetic personal appeal: *"Please* pay attention."

A third possibility is to attract attention. Television advertising has probably exhausted the possibilities. The creators of television advertising assume that people attend to anything that is loud, bright, colorful, endearing, amusing, sudden, strange, or puzzling—or that they will do so at least once, if they are exposed to it many times. Textbooks are often constructed on similar principles, involving the use of colored pictures and intriguing titles and subtitles. Unfortunately, such textbooks have a basic fault: they do not teach students to pay attention to unattractive things. Computers have made it altogether too easy to attract the attention of students, and the need to teach students to pay attention is often neglected, as Julie Vargas has pointed out (1986).

Students pay attention when doing so has reinforcing consequences. Compare a typical classroom with a roomful of bingo players. No one tells bingo players to pay attention, nor are the cards or counters made particularly attractive. The players look and listen carefully for a very good reason: reinforcing consequences follow only when they do so. Well-constructed programs have the same effect. Children who are said to have a short attention span will watch a western on television without taking their eyes off the screen. A book that is not attractive as an object will hold the reader if the writer has filled it with reinforcing things.

Not everything we want to teach can be programmed, but contrived reinforcing contingencies are still useful in the preparation stage. How, for example, can we teach the appreciation of art, music, or literature? Perhaps another story will be helpful.

In the early 1950s two of my students came to me with a problem. They owned several good pieces of modern art with which they had decorated their room, but they had now acquired a roommate who wanted to put a Harvard banner on the wall and a sports trophy or two on the mantelpiece. That would spoil the atmosphere. Did I see any reason why they should not use some of the techniques I had described in my course to teach their roommate to enjoy modern art? I told them I saw no objection, provided they agreed to tell the roommate afterward what they had done.

They began by paying little or no attention to him unless he asked about their paintings or sculptures. They gave a party and bribed a young woman to ask the roommate about these art objects and to hang on his every word. They sent his name to Boston galleries, and he began to receive announcements of shows. A month later they reported some progress: the roommate had asked them to go with him to the Boston Museum of Fine Arts. They went, and when they saw him looking at a picture that he seemed especially to like, they dropped a $5 bill on the floor. He looked down and found the bill. Before another month had passed, they came to show me the first modern painting painted by their roommate!

Recently, I learned that one of the students was living in New York City, and I phoned to ask him about the project. Had they ever told their roommate what they had done? No, he was sorry, they had not. What had happened to the roommate? He was not sure, but he had run across him recently in the Museum of Modern Art! Perhaps my students had no right to intervene in the life of their roommate in that fashion. I think they should at least have told him what they had done. But they had taught him to enjoy modern art, and he was apparently still enjoying it 30 years later. Of course, they had used irrelevant reinforcers. Art is not something worth knowing about simply because you can talk about it to attractive people or find money on the floor of a museum. But that was part of the preparation stage. The paintings and sculptures took over soon enough.

Suppose the roommate had been required to take a course in art appreciation—or had taken one as a "gut" course to remain eligible for a team. How would the instructor have induced him to look at paintings until the reinforcers the artists put into them could have their effect? Traditionally, the instructor would have asked him to answer questions about artists, schools of art, periods, subjects, theories, and so on. Answering those questions would have little more to do with the *enjoyment* of art than the reinforcers my students used. And suppose the instructor had run across such an unwilling student 30 years later in a museum of art. Would he not have been pleased that his teaching had been so successful?

Consequences that are possibly irrelevant must also be used to induce students to read books and to listen to music, until the very different consequences that writers put into their books and that composers and performers put into their music can have their effect. These are the consequences that are eventually "appreciated."

Teachers also go too far in trying to make the preparation stage of learning resemble daily life when, rather than tell students the facts of science, they ask students to discover these facts for themselves. That is how scientists go about their work in the real world, and what is learned in this manner is no doubt a more genuine kind of knowledge. But using apparatus and methods prescribed by a teacher is not really making a discovery. Indeed, this process is not very different from "discovering" the facts of science in a textbook. The discovery approach may help students enjoy "a sense of what learning is all about," and they may find experimenting more interesting than reading, but it is impossible to learn very much science in this way. Only by designing their own apparatus and working out their own methods will students learn much about making discoveries, and that is very rarely done. Good research practice is a subject in its own right, to be taught as such.

It is also a mistake to try to make the preparation stage "creative." A recent article in *Science* reported that only 10% of all scientists had done creative work, a fact that the author explained by saying that only 10% of scientists "possessed creativity." It would be much more important to know how they were said to acquire creativity. People who discover or create are behaving in ways that—by definition—cannot have been taught. But preparing to discover or create is feasible. The key word in Darwin's title was *origin*. The origin of millions of species was to be found not in an act of creation, but in the selection of otherwise unrelated variations. Truly creative individuals, if any exist at all, behave in ways that are selected by reinforcement, but variations must occur to be selected. Some variations may be accidental, but students can learn to increase the number and, in that sense, to be more creative. Like all the creative people of the past, however, they must first be taught something to be creative *with*.

Education is primarily concerned with the transmission of the culture, and that means the transmission of what is already known. Educators have turned to discovery and creativity in an effort to interest their students, but good contingencies of reinforcement do that in a much more profitable way.

◆ PART THREE ◆

Personal Issues

CHAPTER 10

Laurence Smith's Behaviorism and Logical Positivism

This is a work of extraordinary scholarship, the result of what must have been a prodigious amount of reading and research. It examines the supposed influence of logical positivism on three neobehaviorists—Clark L. Hull, Edward C. Tolman, and B. F. Skinner. I review it here in spite of the possibility of bias, in part because the account is so full and so factual that bias is scarcely possible, and because I can add a few details from my own experience. I knew Tolman and Hull well over a period of more than 20 years, and a few personal comments may be helpful.

Smith's book is in part the story of a remarkable confrontation, not only of schools of thought but of people. There have been other political and religious migrations, but few as well documented as the flight of European scholars to America under the whip of Nazism. Among those who came were scholars and scientists of many kinds, but the resulting network of philosophers and psychologists was particularly intricate. Herbert Feigl, the first member of the Vienna Circle to use the term *logical positivism* in print, came to the University of Iowa, where Sigmund Koch, who would write extensively about Hull, was his student. Karl Bühler, though not an intimate of the Circle, moved from Vienna to a small Catholic college in Minnesota, and his student, Gustave Bergman, was for many years closely associated with Kenneth Spence, the best known of Hull's students, also at Iowa. Egan Brunswik went to Berkeley and worked closely with Tolman. Feigl came to Minnesota, where he and I became close friends, although, as he put it, we continued to "cultivate our own gardens." (He was one of a group of friends who came once a week to hear parts of *Walden Two* as I wrote them. Another friend who came, Paul Meehl, would join Kenneth MacCorquodale in writing an important paper on Tolman's "intervening variables.")

In spite of these and many other contacts, I think Smith is right in saying that the "behaviorist-logical positivist alliance was generally much more limited in scope than is commonly supposed" (p. 301). Indeed, I do not believe it was an alliance at all, and, hence, not quite accurately called a "failed alliance."

The book begins with an excellent chapter on "The logical positivist view of science." It was a blend of Fragean logicism and Machian empiricism. (Smith cites Willard van Orman Quine's critique of logical positivism along behavioristic lines, and it may be worth noting that, as an undergraduate at Oberlin, Quine took a course that used Watson's *Psychology from the Standpoint of a Behaviorist* as text.)

Of the three neobehaviorists, Hull most actively promoted a connection with logical positivism. As Smith points out, the assassination of Moritz Schlick weakened the Circle, and the logical positivists turned to the Unity of Science movement. Hull attended the Third International Congress for the Unity of Science in Paris in 1937, was one of the organizers of the Congress in 1939, and gave a paper at the meeting in 1941 at the University of Chicago. In that paper he spoke of the

> striking and significant similarity between the physicalism doctrine of the logical positivists and the approach characteristic of the American behaviorism, originating in the work of J. B. Watson. Intimately related to both of the above movements are the pragmatism of Peirce, James, and Dewey on the one hand, and the operationism of Bridgman, Boring, and Stevens, on the other. These several methodological movements, together with the pioneering experimental work of Pavlov and the other Russian reflexologists are, I believe, uniting to produce in America a behavioral discipline which will be a full-blown natural science. (p. 192)

At various times Hull invited to the Institute of Human Relations at Yale Otto Neurath, J. H. Woodger, Arne Naess, and Gustave Bergman. As Smith points out, however, Hull's own logic was closer to John Dewey's *Logic, the Theory of Inquiry*. His *Principles of Behavior* shows few signs of logical positivism.

In his senior year at M.I.T., Tolman read William James and thought of becoming a philosopher, but chose psychology instead. At Harvard, a seminar with E. B. Holt introduced him to neorealism, a position confirmed for him by Ralph Barton Perry's attack on the idealism of James Royce and by Perry's emphasis on docility and purposiveness. Tolman would continue to use *docile* in Perry's sense of "teachable" and to speak of purpose throughout his life.

Laurence Smith's Behaviorism and Logical Positivism

Neorealism, as Smith says, left Tolman in an embarrassing position. Could purposes and cognitions be seen in the behavior of another organism or were they internal "determiners" of behavior? His equivocation was clear in *Purposive Behavior in Animals and Men*. "Within a single paragraph," Smith points out, "he describes purposes and cognitions 'as immanent' in behavior . . . and on the other hand as 'determinants' or 'causes' of behavior that are 'invented' or 'inferred' by observers."

By 1935, however, Tolman had clarified his position on intervening variables, and Smith attributes the change to his sabbatical year (1933–1934) in Vienna: "His pronouncements about intervening variables in the period immediately after his trip had much the flavor of Carnap's approach. Instead of psychological laws in general, he spoke of functional relations between antecedent conditions and dependent behavior" (p. 117). I believe there is something missing in that account. In 1931, Tolman taught Summer School at Harvard. There were only a few summer school students in those days, and Fred S. Keller and I attended his classes. I am afraid we took an unfair part in the discussions. I spent a good deal of time with Tolman alone. I had taken my degree and was working on rate of ingestion and of food-reinforced lever-pressing in white rats. Later that year I sent Tolman a copy of my paper "The concept of the reflex in the description of behavior" (1931), the major part of my thesis, and he wrote that he had read it with excitement and had discussed it with his seminar.

That paper contained the equation:

$$R = f(S, A)$$

where R represents response, S stimulus, and A "any condition affecting reflex strength." One such condition was the deprivation with which, in another part of my thesis, I identified *drive;* another was conditioning. In the paper which Smith says shows Carnap's influence, Tolman gives the equation:

$$B = f(S, H, T, P)$$

where B represents behavior, S stimulus conditions, H hereditary make-up, T past training (my "conditioning"), and P appetite or aversion (my "drive"). R. S. Woodworth later pointed to the similarity of the equations. In addition to the stimulus, I had called the conditions of which reflex strength was a function "third variables," but Tolman called them "intervening." That may have been the point at which the experimental analysis of behavior parted company from what would become cognitive psychology.

As Smith makes clear, the professional careers of Hull, born in 1884, and Tolman, born in 1886, were well advanced before the hey-day of logical positivism. Born roughly 20 years later (in 1904), I came to Watson by way of Bertrand Russell, who was sympathetic with logical positivism and close to a near-member of the Circle, Ludwig Wittgenstein. As Smith shows, however, my debt was to the empiricism of Ernst Mach. If logical positivism can be said to have begun with the first issue of *Erkenntnis*, I was far enough along in my own career to become a charter subscriber, as I was to its American equivalent *Philosophy of Science*. I was already working on my *Verbal Behavior* when I heard Quine's lectures on Carnap's *Logische Syntax*. (I would later see Carnap when he was staying with the Feigls in Minneapolis, bedridden with a serious back problem.)

Carnap raised the question of what we could say about a robot that behaved like a person, and that sounded like behaviorism, but I disagreed about what could be done with references to ideas, sensations, feelings, and other so-called states of mind. The logical positivists, like some methodological behaviorists (and Boring and Stevens), acknowledged the existence of a mind but ruled references to it out of science because they could not be confirmed by a second person. I preferred radical behaviorism, which accepted the existence of private states, but as states of the body, the study of which should be left to physiology. Data obtained through introspection would not suffice for a science because the privacy made it impossible to learn to introspect them accurately.

Smith's convincing demonstration that logical positivism contributed little to the neobehaviorists, although the announced topic of his book, is one of its less important contributions. Much has been written recently about the history of behaviorism. Gerald Zuriff's *Behaviorism: A Conceptual Reconstruction* (1985) is a general survey. Robert A. Boakes's *From Darwin to Behaviorism: Psychology and the Minds of Animals* (1984) brings the story up to 1930. Smith has carried on from there.

In the 1930s behaviorism trifurcated. Although, as a behaviorist, Tolman thought his intervening variables replaced mental processes, they have been taken over by cognitive psychologists as elements of mind. Hull's intervening variables began as logical constructions but became more and more neurological. (But only in theory. Karl Lashley, an early behaviorist who remained close to Watson even after Watson's departure from the field, went straight to the nervous system itself. His best-known student, Donald Hebb, did not call himself a behaviorist. Untouched by logical positivism, Lashley and Hebb are naturally not mentioned in this book.) I differed from both Tolman and Hull by following a strictly Machian line, in which behavior was analyzed as a subject matter in its own right as a function of environmental variables without reference to

Laurence Smith's Behaviorism and Logical Positivism

either mind or the nervous system. That was the line that Jacques Loeb (1916) had taken, although the only facts Loeb marshalled in support of it were tropisms, in which I was not interested. (Loeb corresponded extensively with Mach.)

In a final chapter, Smith discusses the reemergence of psychologism, especially in philosophical theories of knowledge. All three neobehaviorists "embarked on careers in psychology with a strong interest in epistemology" but "their psychologizing of the knowledge process placed a deep gulf between their indigenous epistemologies and the epistemological views of the logical positivists" (p. 321). Smith seems to feel that the neobehaviorists never reached an adequate understanding of their own behavior as scientists. Although all three anticipated the "new image of scientific knowledge," Smith says that "only some of their notions of science continue to be fruitful . . . It is unlikely that any of the specific formulations of Tolman, Hull, or Skinner will figure in current or future versions of the new image—if for no other reason than that they do not represent the latest developments even in their traditions" (p. 321). I do not think the story is quite finished, however. The chapters on "Logical and Scientific Verbal Behavior" and "Thinking" in my *Verbal Behavior* were, I think, steps in the right direction, and current explorations of the distinction between rule-governed and contingency-shaped behavior are certainly relevant. Some Zuriff, Boakes, or Smith of the future will have to carry the story forward.

◆ CHAPTER 11 ◆

A New Preface to Beyond Freedom and Dignity

W hen *Beyond Freedom and Dignity* was first published, in 1971, the reviews were mixed, in the sense not only that some critics liked it and some did not, but also that those who liked it had reservations and those who disliked it usually thought it had some merit. Few questioned the importance of the problems it discussed. Certainly more should be done to preserve the resources of the world, maintain a habitable environment, bring the population under control, and prevent a nuclear war. But would a science of behavior be of much help?

Many critics said that the book lacked substance. I should have described the science in greater detail and explained how it could be used. It is true that I was thinking of a particular kind of science, which was probably not familiar to many readers and a sketch of which might have helped, but I was asking why no behavioral science was being used, no matter what the kind.

A dedication to freedom and dignity was among the reasons. If people were actually free to do as they pleased, even if only occasionally, a science of behavior was impossible, and some critics dismissed my book out of hand on that ground. But I was not arguing the issue of determinism. Whether or not one was actually free had little to do with whether one *felt* free, and the historical struggle for freedom was a struggle for the feeling, not the fact. Similarly, whether one could justly claim credit for one's accomplishments had little to do with one's feeling of dignity or worth. What lay beyond freedom and dignity was the future of a world in which those and other valued feelings could still be enjoyed.

Some of the critics who were not disturbed by the issue of determinism argued that a science of behavior was impossible for another reason. Behavior might be the result of all that had happened during the

113

genetic and personal histories of the behaving person, but those histories were not only out of reach, they would be much too complex to be analyzed if they were accessible. Other critics, however, complained that a science of behavior was altogether too feasible. Behavior was being controlled all the time—by governments, economic systems, and religions—and the improved control that would follow from a technology of behavior was not an idle dream but a serious threat. Who would use it and to what end? Who would control human behavior, and who would control the controllers? *Quis custodiet ipsos custodes?* Who is to control the authorities?

I think that that question can be answered by translating *quis* as *what* rather than *who*. For thousands of years it has been believed that human behavior is the expression of feelings and states of mind. Something happens inside a person and behavior then follows. Perhaps what happens inside will eventually be observed with the methods and instruments of physiology, but a kind of direct observation is already possible. The human body is a unique subject matter; the observer is the thing observed. Mental processes can be felt or "introspected." Philosophers have practiced introspection for a very long time, but they have never reached any general agreement on what they have seen. No feeling or state of mind has ever been unambiguously identified or defined without referring to its antecedents or consequences, and they are not what is seen through introspection.

Why we have feelings and states of mind is a different question, seldom asked. Of course, some of the things that have happened to us are obviously relevant. We may eat because we feel hungry, for example, but we feel hungry because we have not recently eaten. Not until well into the 20th century, however, was behavior traced directly to what had happened, rather than by way of intervening states. The change was due in part to the theory of evolution. The behavior of nonhuman animals was once explained on the human model: Animals had feelings and ideas and behaved accordingly. Evolutionary theory gave a different explanation: the ways in which animals behaved had been selected by their contribution to the survival of the species. Survival is only one kind of selective consequence, however. Most of what we do can be traced to two other kinds, much closer to the issues in this book. A brief review seems necessary, especially if I am to "add substance" to my argument.

OPERANT CONDITIONING

Natural selection prepares an organism only for a future that resembles the selecting past. That is a serious limitation, and to some extent it was corrected by the evolution of a process through which a different kind of consequence could select additional behavior during the lifetime of the individual. The process is called operant conditioning and the selecting consequence a reinforcer.

Both natural selection and operant conditioning have been slow to make their way as scientific explanations because they conflict with well-established views. Selection replaces purpose, for example. The hand is not designed "for the purpose of grasping things"; hands grasp things well because variations in structure have been selected when they improved grasping, a contribution to survival. People do not grasp things in given ways "with the purpose of holding them firmly"; they grasp them in ways in which they *have* held them firmly, a reinforcing consequence. Selection also has no place for a plan (in both natural selection and operant conditioning, variations have no prior relevance to the consequences that select them) or for an initiator or creator. Alternative religious views of the origin of species no longer trouble biologists, but the role of a creative mind in the origin of behavior is still a challenge to behavior analysts.

THE EVOLUTION OF CULTURAL PRACTICES

Operant conditioning, too, has its limitations. It greatly extends the range of behavior, but it also prepares only for a future that resembles the selecting past. Moreover, only a small repertoire could be acquired during a single lifetime through operant conditioning alone. Those limitations were corrected in turn by the evolution of processes through which organisms received help from other members of their species. When one animal imitates another, for example, it sometimes profits from the consequences of what the other is doing. The advantages are felt in both natural selection and operant conditioning, and they are particularly important when the consequences are rare.

Let us say, for example, that by some lucky accident a monkey cracks a particular kind of nut it has never cracked before and that the meat proves reinforcing. The monkey will be likely to crack that kind of nut in the same way again. By imitating its behavior, other monkeys will come under the control of the same contingencies in spite of their rarity.

When animals have begun to imitate each other, conditions prevail for the natural selection of modeling. If, for example, there are advantages to the species when young birds imitate their parents and thus fly sooner, additional advantages follow when the parents fly in easily imitated ways where their young can see them. Operant modeling, however, appears to be exclusively human and, even then, is not readily explained. Although parents may show their children how to do things because, for example, the children then need less help, that consequence is deferred. How it can affect behavior is a question of which we shall meet other examples.

Modeling is a way of showing another organism what to do. It primes behavior in the sense of evoking it for the first time and thus exposing it to potential contingencies of reinforcement. Telling is a much more effective kind of priming. Vocal behavior has, of course, many advantages: Animals can respond vocally when they are busy with other things and hear when they are not looking. In the human species, however, vocal behavior is also shaped and maintained by its reinforcing consequences. This is an exclusive feature which gives the species a special advantage and may, in fact, explain all its extraordinary achievements.

One way to tell a person what to do is to give advice—either in the form of an injunction, possibly with an allusion to a consequence ("Twist the key slowly; it works better that way") or as a description of a contingency of reinforcement ("The key works better when twisted slowly"). We sometimes add a reinforcement of our own: we show someone how to twist the key and say "Right" when he does so. What eventually reinforces his behavior is not our "Right"; it is what is gained from turning the key in a special way.

Customary relations between behavior and its consequences are often described in proverbs and maxims, either as injunctions ("Count to 10 in anger," with the implication, "and you may avoid doing something you would regret") or descriptions of the contingencies ("A soft answer turneth away wrath"). Complex contingencies are described in rules and laws, especially the rules for effective action that we call the laws of science.

That kind of helping works to the advantage of those who are helped, but contingencies of reinforcement are more often arranged because they work to the advantage of those who arrange them. When, for example, we ask a subordinate to do something for us and imply an aversive consequence if he refuses, we are freed from doing it ourselves. Three great institutions arrange contingencies of reinforcement primarily because of the consequences for the institutions. Negative reinforcers are the staple of governments, which use them either as punishment to suppress unwanted behavior ("No parking") or, more often, as negative reinforcers to strengthen wanted behavior ("Pay your taxes and avoid a fine").

Such an explicit use of contingencies is exclusively human. (The dominance hierarchies of nonverbal species are due to natural selection.)

A *New Preface to* Beyond Freedom and Dignity

Positive reinforcers (capital) are the staple of business and industry. People are paid when they work or hand over goods. The contingencies require verbal devices, such as prices or contracts, which are beyond the reach of other species. Some religions are essentially systems of ethics; they prime social behavior which may prove to have reinforcing consequences. Some describe consequences said to follow in another world, the contingencies usually being under partial control of authorities in this one.

This account of how people modify the behavior of other people is oversimplified, but it will help in discussing present issues. The term *cultural evolution* is often used very loosely. According to the *Columbia History of the World* (1972), for example, "when we talk about human evolution, we are dealing with two different kinds of processes: the evolution of the human body and the evolution of human behavior . . . . The latter, cultural evolution, is a bio-social process that falls within the domain of archaeologists and cultural anthropologists" (p. 38). But a "bio-social process," such as "sociobiology," moves too quickly from the evolution of species to the evolution of cultures, passing over a very necessary link between them, the operant behavior of the individual.

Consider the practice of quenching a fire. Many thousands of years ago someone must for the first time have accidentally thrown water on a threatening fire and watched it go out. If that consequence was reinforcing, the behavior would have been repeated on similar occasions. But such occasions would have been rare. Water would not often be at hand when a fire threatened (and only much later could having it at hand have reinforced storing it for use). Eventually, however, someone would quench fires often enough, and in such a conspicuous way, that others would imitate the behavior and come under the control of the same rare contingencies. The practice would spread more rapidly when others were shown how to quench a fire, and still more rapidly when they were told.

The origin and transmission of a cultural practice are thus plausibly explained as the joint product of natural selection and operant conditioning. A culture, however, is the set of practices characteristic of a group of people, and it is selected by a different kind of consequence, its contribution to the survival of the group. That is an important point. Although the controlled use of fire may contribute to the survival of the culture of which it is a part, that consequence is too remote to reinforce the behavior of any member of the group.

The "terrifying problems" mentioned in the first paragraph of this book are also consequences too remote to serve either as punishments to suppress the behavior that is causing trouble or as negative reinforcers to strengthen behavior that will provide a remedy. The first nuclear weapon was designed by scientists and built by workers who were paid by a government that was acting under the threat of a prolonged and destructive war. The fact that a war in which both sides used nuclear weapons would almost certainly destroy the world as we know it was too remote a consequence to override the immediate gain. People produce and consume vast quantities of goods just because goods are "good"— that is, reinforcing, but the fact that the materials of which they are composed, in both agriculture and industry, will eventually be exhausted and that the by-products of their use will irreversibly foul the environment are consequences too remote to have any current effect. People have children for many reasons, but the fact that further growth of the world's population will magnify all our problems is still another threatening consequence too remote and ineffective to affect behavior.

When I wrote this book I thought that we could correct for the weakness of remote consequences simply by creating current surrogates to serve in their place. Our treatment of cigarette smoking is a miniature model of what might be done. Smoking is reinforced either positively by the so-called pleasures of smoking or negatively by relief from withdrawal symptoms. Damaging effects on the smoker's health are adventitious consequences, too remote to punish smoking. When those effects had been discovered, however, something could be done. Smokers could be advised to stop smoking and warned of the consequences ("Smoking can be dangerous to your health"). Advice is seldom enough, however. Consequences which have not yet occurred have no effect. Advice about predicted consequences is usually taken only if taking comparable advice has been reinforced, and that is seldom, if ever, the case when the predicted consequences are remote. Another possibility, however, is to contrive immediate consequences having the effect the remote ones would have if they were immediate. Reinforce not smoking ("Thank you for not smoking"), and enthusiastically commend those who have stopped. Punish smoking with criticism, complaints, restrictions on where one may smoke, and heavy taxes on cigarettes.

On a very much larger scale I thought we could find current surrogates for the remote consequences which now threaten the world. Give people reasons for having only a few children or none at all and remove the reasons why they often have so many. Promote ways of life which are less consuming and less polluting. Reduce aggression and the likelihood of war by taking a smaller share of the wealth of the world. A science of behavior would spawn the technology needed to make changes of that sort, and I thought the science was aborning.

Design is only a first step, however. Designs must be put into effect, and only by those who can do so effectively. That means governments, religions, and economic enterprises, which control most of the conditions under which we all live. They, however, are under the control of consequences affecting their own survival, which are much less remote and hence more powerful than the survival of the species. Moreover, the effects of these consequences are usually in conflict with it. For example, the legislator who sponsored a proposal to lower the birthrate, limit personal possessions, and weaken national and religious commitments would soon lose the power to sponsor anything. Business and industry cannot turn to the production of goods and services which will have fewer harmful consequences but will be less reinforcing to those who buy them. Religious leaders must make sure that their advice will be taken, and communicants will not take it if taking other advice has cost them reinforcers. Those leaders whose advice concerns consequences in another world must treat this world as expendable.

Can some use be made of the fact that the survival of institutions is largely a matter of competition? Governments compete with other governments, religions with other religions or unbelievers, and businesses and industries with other businesses and industries. A world government, a truly catholic religion, and a global economy would reduce that kind of waste, unless they challenged each other. A combination of all three in some kind of world communism would raise the specter of unrestrained control. When space and other necessities are in short supply, evolution *is* competition.

It was Juvenal who asked *quis custodiet ipsos custodes?* and he was discussing the problem of the jealous husband: if he puts his wife in the hands of guards, she will be unfaithful with the guards. As I have noted, we can answer Juvenal's question by translating *quis* as *what* rather than *who*. For example, it could be said that a jealous husband could find his answer in loyalty. Loyal guards (or a loyal wife) would solve his problem. But people do not behave loyally because they are loyal, and the conditions under which they *are* loyal are the conditions under which they *behave* loyally. (Whether saying so destroys loyalty as a trait of character is not unlike other questions asked in this book. Certainly, we should not call a guard loyal who was extremely well paid, could be severely punished, and was being closely watched. Should we not say the same about any trait of character if we knew all the relevant facts?) The question is this: *Under what conditions* will those who have the power to control human behavior use it in ways that promise a better future?

It is probably significant that I wrote this book near the end of a decade in which young people were challenging all three major institutions—government by trashing, stealing, and calling the police pigs, business and industry by refusing to work and begging for the things they needed, and organized religion by turning to the unorganized forms of the East. It was a kind of nonaggressive anarchy. It survived for a time, only because it was treated with remarkable leniency. It could not survive long, because its followers found no replacements for the institutions they abandoned. In that decade, however, my book *Walden Two* came to life. Published in 1948, it was soon on the point of going out of print. In the 1960s, however, its sales rose exponentially. The community it described was not a hippie commune, but it was free of institutions. The functions of government, economics, and religion were taken over by face-to-face personal control.

As a pilot experiment in the design of a culture, a community has the advantage that its survival is always a question, and practices are closely watched for their bearing on the answer. One of the things salvaged from the 1960s was a greater concern for the future of the world and its inhabitants. Fortunately, we now have better ways of expressing that concern. Ecologists and other kinds of scientists follow current trends closely and make increasingly reliable predictions about the future of the earth. Teachers and the media tell more people about what is likely to happen. Governmental, religious, and economic practices are undoubtedly beginning to be affected. It is possible, in short, that we are witnessing the evolution of a true "fourth estate," composed of scientists, scholars, teachers, and the media. If it can remain free of governments, religions, and economic enterprises, it may provide current surrogates for the remoter consequences of our behavior. It could be the *quis* that will control the controllers. Nothing short of a better understanding of human behavior will solve our problems, and I still believe that this means better science and technology. Whether they will evolve in time is the ultimate question. Those who are unhappy about scientific solutions sometimes assure us that we shall solve our problems in other ways when they are bad enough, when the immediate consequences are no longer reinforcing and the remoter ones have been sampled. But it is in the nature of overpopulation, the exhaustion and pollution of the environment, and a nuclear war that "bad enough" is a point of no return.

CHAPTER 12

The Behavior of Organisms *at 50*

I have lived my professional life by decades. It was 60 years ago, in 1928, that I arrived at Harvard as a graduate student in psychology. Behaviorism was then only 15 years old. Ten years later, in 1938, I published *The Behavior of Organisms* and 10 years after that, in 1948, *Walden Two*. Things were then taken out of my hands, but still by decades. Nineteen fifty-eight saw the first issue of *The Journal of the Experimental Analysis of Behavior*, the title reminiscent of the subtitle of *The Behavior of Organisms*, and 10 years later the behavioral engineering of *Walden Two* moved from fiction to real life in the first issue of *The Journal of Applied Behavior Analysis*. Of all the anniversaries one is likely to celebrate in a lifetime the 50th is the golden one, and that is why this chapter is about *The Behavior of Organisms* and how it looks to me after half a century.

First, however, a word about sources. The commitment to behaviorism that sent me from college to graduate study in psychology was at the time no better supported than my commitment in high school to the theory that Francis Bacon wrote the works of Shakespeare. I had taken my college degree in English Language and Literature with a minor in Romance Languages and was hoping to be a writer. An important book for writers at that time was *The Meaning of Meaning* by C. K. Ogden and I. A. Richards (1923). Bertrand Russell reviewed it for a literary magazine called the *Dial*, to which I subscribed, and in a footnote he acknowledged his indebtedness to "Dr. Watson" whose recent book *Behaviorism* (1925) he found "massively impressive." I bought Watson's book and liked its campaigning style. Later I bought Russell's *Philosophy* (1927), in which he treated a few mentalistic terms in a behavioristic way. Although I had never had a course in psychology, I became an instant behaviorist. When a book called *The Religion Called Behaviorism* appeared, I wrote a critical review and sent it to *The Saturday Review of Literature*. (Fortunately, the review was never published.)

Philip Pauly's *Controlling Life* (1987) has reminded me of an earlier source of *The Behavior of Organisms*. I wanted to study the behavior of an organism quite apart from any reference to mental life, and that was Watson, but I also wanted to avoid references to the nervous system, and that was Jacques Loeb. Loeb was a German biologist who had come to America and, like Watson, had come into contact with the Functionalist School at the University of Chicago. (Later, at the Rockefeller Institute, he would become the model for Max Gottlieb in Sinclair Lewis's *Arrowsmith*.) My biology professor at Hamilton College had shown me Loeb's *Comparative Physiology of the Brain and Comparative Psychology* (1900) and later his *The Organism as a Whole* (1916), and at Harvard I found myself in the biological laboratories of W. J. Crozier, Loeb's major disciple, who, as Loeb was said to have done, "resented the nervous system." I don't believe I coined the term *radical behaviorism*, but when asked what I mean by it, I have always said, "the philosophy of a science of behavior treated as a subject matter in its own right apart from internal explanations, mental *or physiological*."

The chapter in *The Behavior of Organisms* on the relevance of the nervous system ends with a quotation from still another source. As Laurence Smith (1987) has shown, logical positivism came too late to influence Tolman, Hull, or me in any important way, but it was itself largely due to an earlier figure, Ernst Mach. My doctoral thesis acknowledged my indebtedness to Mach's *The Science of Mechanics* (1915), and it is probably relevant that, although Loeb and Mach never met, they corresponded. (I owned a copy of Mach's *Erkenntnis und Irrtum* but it was in German, and I doubt that I got much out of it at the time.)

A friend, Cuthbert Daniel, who would become a distinguished statistician, put me on to another man in the same tradition. Daniel had come to Harvard to work with P. W. Bridgman, and he told me to read Bridgman's *The Logic of Modern Physics* (1928). So far as I can now identify them, those were the sources of my theoretical position in *The Behavior of Organisms*.

Watson's famous manifesto (1913) begins: "Psychology as the behaviorist views it is a purely objective experimental branch of natural science. Its theoretical goal is the prediction and control of behavior." Those are carefully written sentences. Psychology is a branch of science. Behaviorism is the philosophy of that science, the way behaviorists view it.

The Behavior of Organisms *at 50*

There were not many examples of the prediction and control of behavior in psychology at that time. Indeed, as the expression of mental life, behavior was beyond control by definition. Biology offered something better. Loeb had preferred the tropism, and it was certainly a beautiful example of control, but very little of the behavior I was interested in could be described as a function of a field of force. Reflexes were closer. With a light shock to the foot of a decerebrate cat, Sir Charles Sherrington (1906) could make its leg flex, and with a bit of food or, significantly, a stimulus frequently paired with food, Pavlov (1927) could make a dog salivate, and that was control. Reflexes, however, were the behavior of only parts of an organism. Like Loeb I wanted to study the behavior of the "organism as a whole."

I built an apparatus in which a white rat ran along a delicately mounted pathway. The forces exerted on the pathway were recorded more or less as Sherrington had recorded the forces exerted by a single muscle on his "torsion-wire myograph." But something else turned up in my experiment. The rat was hungry and got a bit of food at the end of each run. I noticed that after it had finished eating it did not always start immediately on another run. The delays in starting seemed to vary in an orderly way, and that suggested another kind of control in the "organism as a whole." After a long series of steps, I found myself recording the rate at which the rat ate pellets of food or got them by pressing a lever.

I recorded the behavior in a cumulative curve, a form of graph not well understood for a long time. It had many advantages. The curve that resulted showed a steady decline in slope, suggesting an orderly process of satiation as the rat ate its daily ration. When I did not let the rat get pellets for a few minutes, it ate more rapidly when they were again available, and the cumulative record rose to meet a rough extrapolation of the earlier part. A rather subtle change in behavior was exposed to view. I doubt that I should have so quickly recognized the process of satiation as such if I had recorded the behavior in any other way.

Changes in the slope of a cumulative record showed changes in what I called the strength of behavior. Reflexes, conditioned and uncon-ditioned, were also said to vary in strength. A flexion reflex was strong if the stimulus elicited a vigorous response. A salivary reflex was strong if the stimulus elicited a great deal of saliva. In other words, reflex strength was measured as the ratio of the magnitudes of stimulus and response. I could not see that such a measure was possible with pressing a lever. In some sense the lever must be acting as a stimulus, but I could not turn it on or off or measure it. The rate at which the rat ate pellets of food or pressed a lever could serve as an alternative, however. Rate of responding has proved, in fact, to be a highly useful dependent variable. In a later paper I could report that it varied usefully over a range of at least 600 to 1.

Rate of responding was also more useful as a measure because it could be said to show the probability that a response would be made at a given time. Nothing of the sort could be said of a reflex, where the stimulus determined whether or not a response was made. Probability simply did not fit the stimulus-response pattern. It was also not an issue in research with mazes, where the question was how an animal learned to find (and hence to know how to find) its way. But I was asking not whether my rat knew how to press a lever to get food, but how strongly it was inclined to press. Later I would ask how that inclination was affected by the presence or absence of a discriminative stimulus.

Two Polish physiologists, Konorski and Miller, were doing experiments rather like mine. They were adding a reinforcing consequence to a reflex. For example, they shocked the foot of a hungry dog and gave it food when its leg flexed. Eventually the leg flexed although the foot was not shocked. They went to Leningrad to tell Pavlov about their experiment, and they sent me a book (written in Polish, but with generous marginal notations added in French). Later they published a paper in English (1935), to which I replied (1935a). I argued that the shock to the foot in their experiment was unnecessary. They could have waited to give food when the dog flexed its leg for any reason whatsoever, and flexion would have been conditioned. The shock served merely to bring out the response so that it could be reinforced. As I would say later, it "primed" the behavior. It was in my reply to Konorski and Miller that I first used the word *operant*.

In 1935 I published a paper called *The Generic Nature of the Concepts of Stimulus and Response* in which I argued that a reflex was not something that could be observed on a given occasion. What was observed was a response, which might not be exactly like responses observed at other times, and it was elicited by a stimulus which might not be quite like other stimuli. (We could not always be sure precisely which of its properties the organism was responding to on a given occasion.) There were defining properties, however, and the orderliness of the observed data told us what they were and established their validity.

The paper was too strongly tied to the concept of the reflex. What I was really worrying about was operant behavior. For example, I was asking questions about a "reflex reserve" (of which more later). Did a single reinforcement always add the same number of responses to the reserve? Did a single unreinforced response always subtract the same number during extinction? A smooth extinction curve, of which I had some beautiful examples, seemed to justify speaking of a unit of behavior in spite of a considerable diversity in the properties of single instances. It was such a unit that I called an *operant*. What was *reinforced* was a response as an instance; what was *strengthened* was an operant—the probability that other responses would occur.

Instead of *operant*, Watson would have said *habit*, and there were no doubt similarities. Running through a maze was not a habit, it was something a rat did because it *had* a habit. That was close to the distinction between an operant as a kind of behavior and an operant response as an instance. Habits could also have been said to vary in strength, although a "strong habit" was not standard usage. A habit was usually nothing more than something an organism did. Precisely how likely it was to do it was seldom an issue.

The main difference between an operant and a habit seemed to be one of size. Pressing a lever could have been called a habit, but so could running through a complicated maze, which was composed of many operants, each with its own stimulus, response, and consequence. An operant was a kind of behavioral atom. True, I could take pressing a lever apart by extinguishing its parts separately (*The Behavior of Organisms*, 1938, p. 102), but even so it was close to a minimal unit.

What remained to be done in a science of behavior seemed clear. I should look for other independent variables and observe their effects. Here are a few of what now seem to me to be important ways in which the research reported in *The Behavior of Organisms* differed from what was being done by others at the same time.

Learning

Contemporary work on animal behavior emphasized learning. Although I had reported satiation curves when rats were pressing a lever to get pellets of food, I had not watched them learn to press. When I turned to the so-called "learning process" directly, the result was surprising. Its significance is still not always recognized. An accident had led me to an important feature of the experiment. Pavlov had taught me the importance of controlling conditions, and I wanted my rats to be as free as possible of disturbances when they first pressed the lever and got food. To accustom them to the experimental box I fed them their daily rations in it for several days. To reduce the disturbing effects of being put into the box, I put them first into a small compartment inside, from which I could silently release them when the experiment began. To prevent any disturbance from the sound of the food dispenser, I dispensed many pellets when the lever was in its lowest position and could not be pressed down. It would be years before I understood what I had thus done. I had unwittingly conditioned the sound of the dispenser as a reinforcer. When that was done, a *single reinforcement* was enough to condition pressing the lever as an operant. There was no learning curve, and hence little to be attributed to a learning process.

Operant conditioning is an abrupt change in the way an organism behaves. The "learning process" supposedly revealed by a learning curve varies with the setting in which the organism is said to learn and with the repertoire the organism brings to the setting. The shape of the curve varies accordingly. I do not think the word *learn* has any useful referent. There is only one entry in the index of *The Behavior of Organisms* under learning, and the text to which it refers is in quotation marks.

Many textbooks in psychology continue to describe operant conditioning as trial-and-error learning. I think Thorndike's experiment on the Law of Effect, clearly an anticipation of operant conditioning, led to that misunderstanding. His cat was "trying" to get out of the puzzle box in the sense that its behavior was due to two kinds of earlier consequences. It was responding as members of its species had, for millions of years, responded to (and gained by escaping from) physical restraint. It was also responding as it had responded, as an individual, to aversive constraints with reinforcing consequences during its lifetime. But one may reinforce almost anything an organism is doing and it will become an operant. The organism need not be trying to do anything. Many of the things Thorndike's cats did could also be called errors in the sense that reinforcing consequences did not follow, but my rats learned from their successes. There was neither trial nor error.

Punishment

Throughout the book I misused the expression *negative conditioning*, but I think the experiments were productive. I did not want to shock my rats and built a device which, as I said, merely slapped their paws when they pressed the lever. When responses were followed by slaps, the rats responded more rapidly for a few moments and then stopped. When responses were "negatively reinforced" in this way for a few minutes at the start of extinction, the rats stopped responding, but once free of slapping they recovered, and by the end of 2 one-hour sessions the extinction curve was essentially where it would have been if no responses had been slapped.

The Behavior of Organisms *at 50*

What I called negative conditioning should, of course, have been called punishment. *Reinforcement* (and its synonym *conditioning*) means to strengthen, but the behavior in my experiment grew weak. A negative reinforcer is properly defined as "a stimulus the *reduction or removal* of which strengthens behavior." If we define a positive reinforcer as a stimulus that strengthens behavior when presented and a negative reinforcer as one that strengthens when removed, then punishment consists of presenting a negative reinforcer (as I had done) or removing a positive one.

The effect of punishment, however, seems reasonably well explained in the book. When a response is followed by, say, a shock, an emotional reaction to the shock is conditioned according to Type S [Pavlovian] conditioning. Approaching the lever elicits such a reaction, which reduces the strength of lever pressing. I could have added that incompatible behavior would also be strengthened by any reduction in such a conditioned aversive stimulus and would oppose the occurrence of the behavior punished.

The Discriminative Stimulus

In mentalistic or cognitive psychology, stimuli are things to be acted upon. We see or perceive them, and the question is how well we do so. A stimulus plays a different role, however, when as a "cue" it tells us *when* to do something (*cue* comes from the Latin *quando*, when) or as a "clue" *what* to do (etymologically the first clue was the thread that led Theseus out of the Labyrinth). The role of the stimulus in operant behavior remained unclear for many years. In my 1935 paper about two types of conditioned reflex and a pseudo type, the stimulus in the pseudo type had a special function, which had appeared in some experiments on discrimination. I had been reinforcing a response every 5 minutes in what I called "periodic reconditioning." I arranged a given reinforcement by dropping a pellet into a food dispenser, to be released when the rat next pressed. But the rat could hear the pellet drop, and it responded immediately afterwards. To correct that fault I built an electrical dispenser with which I could set up a reinforcement silently by closing a switch.

The response to the sound of the pellet was worth studying in its own right, however. In place of the sound, I would use a light. I called it an S Dee—a discriminative stimulus. When a response was reinforced only in the presence of the light as an S Dee, the rat responded slowly in its absence (which, unfortunately, I called S Delta, hard to print) but responded immediately when the light came on. The light could have been called a cue or clue, of course, and cognitive psychologists, if there had been any, might have said that it conveyed information about when to press the lever. It was simpler, however, to say only that an operant was stronger in the presence of any stimulus in the presence of which it had been reinforced.

That avoided speculating about processes. It is often said, for example, that Pavlov's dog associated the bell with food but, as I have often pointed out, it was Pavlov who associated them in the sense of putting them together, making a society of them. All we can say of the dog is that reinforcement changed it in such a way that it responded to the bell as it had responded to the food. The same mistake is made in speaking of an operant discrimination. When a pigeon pecks any picture in which a person appears, but does not peck any in which there are no persons, it is said to have formed a concept, but it is the experimenter who has done so by arranging the contingencies. (For that matter, it is misleading to say that a pigeon "forms a discrimination." The pigeon is changed in such a way that it responds more often to settings which have certain properties.)

The rat's own behavior presumably generated discriminative stimuli, and they seemed to explain the performances appearing under "periodic reconditioning." When I first reinforced responses intermittently, a small extinction curve followed each reinforcement, but the curves soon fused, and for some time the rat responded at a steady rate. Stimuli from its own behavior, however, (together with stimuli from other events occurring as time passed) soon began to have an effect. Eventually the rate dropped to a low value immediately after reinforcement and then steadily increased until another reinforcement occurred. The overall rate under "periodic reconditioning" became a useful dependent variable. In the experiments reported in *The Behavior of Organisms* it varied with the period of reconditioning and with the level of deprivation. It has been widely used to study the effects of other "third variables."

When I began to reinforce the last of a fixed number of responses, stimulation generated by a given number proved to be more powerful than stimulation due to the passage of time, and the rat began to respond rapidly. A very large number of responses could be "added to the reserve" with a single occasional reinforcement.

Differentiation and Shaping

Topographical features of operant behavior—for example, the speed or energy with which a response was executed—were also presumably due to reinforcing consequences, and the contingencies needed to be studied.

The Behavior of Organisms *at 50*

Suppose we want a rat to press a lever very hard. We cannot reinforce especially hard responses, because they do not occur, but we can take advantage of spontaneous variations. We begin by reinforcing all responses and measuring, say, the force with which they are made. The measured forces will be distributed about a mean. If we select particularly forceful responses for further reinforcement, a new distribution will emerge in which some responses will be more forceful than any in the first distribution. We can then select a still harder response for reinforcement. Eventually we reach a distribution about an extremely forceful mean. The origin of behavior is thus very much like the origin of species. When particular features of an operant are strengthened by differential reinforcement, new features come into existence as variations. It is in the nature of behavior, as it is in the nature of a genetic trait, that there are variations, and that new behavior and new genomes emerge when variations are selected by their consequences.

The Behavior of Organisms contains an example in which the topography of behavior is shaped in a rather similar way. A rat learned to release a marble from a rack, carry it to a slot, and drop it in. The necessary contingencies were programmed by changing the apparatus in small steps. (It was only later, on Project Pigeon, that we discovered how much more expeditiously we could shape complex behavior by operating a food dispenser with a hand switch.)

The Nervous System

The chapter called "Behavior and the Nervous System" contains no new data. It is rather contentious. Sentences begin with expressions such as, "What I am here contending . . . ," "I am asserting . . . ," or "What I am arguing. . . . " That was probably my reaction to the open contempt for psychology shown by physiologists at the Harvard Medical School (except for that gentle man, Walter B. Cannon) and at Minnesota. A declaration of independence from physiology was essential to "radical behaviorism," however, and I argued the case strenuously.

In my thesis I had pointed out that Sherrington never saw the action of the synapse about which he spoke so confidently, and I could convert its supposed properties into laws of behavior. Sherrington's book was not about the integrative action of the nervous system; it was about the behavior of part of a decerebrate cat. Nor had Pavlov seen "the physiological activity of the cerebral cortex" mentioned in the subtitle of his book. The book was about the control of salivation.

I am afraid my argument that behavior should be recognized as a subject matter in its own right has been misunderstood. I have never questioned the importance of physiology or in particular brain science or its relevance to behavior. What is happening inside the skin of an organism is part of its behavior, but it does not explain what the organism does in the space around it until it has been explained in turn. If the nervous system (or, better, the whole organism) is the product of the evolution of the species and of what has happened to the individual during its lifetime, and if what the organism does is the product of current processes in the nervous system (or, better, the whole organism), then what the organism does is the product of natural selection and of what has happened to the individual, and that is what ethology and the experimental analysis of behavior are all about.

We are likely to search the brain (or mind?) for explanations of behavior when no other explanation is available. The more we learn about the environmental variables of which behavior is a function, however, the less likely we are to search. We can predict and control behavior without knowing anything about what is happening inside. A complete account will nevertheless require the joint action of both sciences, each with its own instruments and methods.

The Behavior of Organisms had its critics, of course, but I thought I could answer most of their complaints. They said my title was wrong, for example. The book was not about organisms; it was about a particular strain of white rat. (But Sherrington's book was about the nervous system *of the cat* and Pavlov's about conditioned reflexes *in the dog*.) Other critics said that the cumulative record was nothing but a subtle way of smoothing data. The curves were indeed often smoother than "learning curves" obtained with mazes, even when scores for many subjects were averaged, but that was scarcely a fault. Critics said that single-organism research left a great deal of "noise" in the data. The data were closer to what organisms actually did, however, and many of them were far from noisy.

The book had more serious faults, of course, which are easier to see from a distance of 50 years. In spite of my insistence that behavior should be studied as a function of external variables apart from any reference to mental or physiological states or processes, I was not yet wholly free of the traditional view. For example, I spoke as if behavior were inside the organism before it came out. A reflex was traditionally said to be "elicited" in the etymological sense of "drawn out." Operant behavior was different, and I tried to emphasize the difference by saying that it was "evoked," in the sense of "called out." (The ethologists would soon be saying "released.") I also said that operant behavior was "emitted," and later I tried to justify that usage by pointing out that the light emitted from a hot filament was not in the filament.

The "reflex reserve" carried the metaphor much further. Conditioning put responses into the reserve, and they came out during extinction.
I designed experiments to find out how many responses a single
reinforcement put in, and I argued that anything that changed the
strength of an operant must change either the size of the reserve or the
relation between it and rate of responding. Within a year after publication
of the book, I abandoned the "reflex reserve," but I should have done so
much sooner. Speculating about internal processes was a violation of a
basic principle. An operant response was not emitted; it simply occurred.

Of course I was also too strongly committed to the "reflex." The
action of a stimulus in "eliciting" a response was a good example of
control, and many behaviorists remained committed to some version of
stimulus-and-response for many years, but according to my experiments,
what happened *after* an organism behaved played a much larger role than
what happened before. Unfortunately I decided to use *reflex* as the word
for any unit of behavior. In doing so, I no doubt contributed to the fact
that you will still find a behavioral analysis called *stimulus-response
psychology.*

The Behavior of Organisms can, I think, be properly evaluated only
by comparing it with the other work that was being done at the time. The
issues of the *Journal of Comparative Psychology* for 1937 and 1938 may be a
fair sample. Roughly 38% of the papers in them were about physiological
variables—brain lesions, drugs, and so on. Roughly 11% would now be
called ethological; they were studies of behavior in the field. Another 11%
were on motivation or emotion. A few, perhaps 5%, were inspired by
Gestalt psychology. The remaining 34% were in the field of my book.
They dealt with Pavlovian conditioning and behavior in mazes and
discrimination boxes. Conditioning involved a certain amount of "prediction and control," but it was the behavior of an organ, not an organism.
Glandular behavior, moreover, was of limited interest. Leg flexion was
studied on the conditioned reflex pattern as an example of skeletal
behavior, but it was again the behavior of a mere organ, and the
experiments usually involved a mixture of respondent and operant
contingencies. What organisms did in mazes and discrimination boxes
was seldom, if ever, treated as a function of manipulable variables. In
short, contemporary animal research was not moving very fast toward
Watson's "theoretical goal" of prediction and control.

Perhaps a book can be said to contain the seeds of what grew out
of it. Although I had said, "Let him extrapolate who will," I was soon
extrapolating. Chronologically, Project Pigeon came first. Our pigeons
never guided any real missiles, but I think they made a contribution to

Personal Issues

the discussion with which *The Behavior of Organisms* ends. In most of my experiments I had used 4 rats; I am not quite sure why. They did not all behave in precisely the same way, and I was once criticized for calling a cumulative record "typical," although I believe I did so on only 4 of the roughly 150 curves in the book. Even when I reported an averaged curve, I almost always gave individual samples and argued that they were more valuable than the average.

Project Pigeon demonstrated my point about statistics beautifully. You cannot put the "average pigeon" into a missile. It must be one real pigeon, and it must behave precisely in a given way under many distracting circumstances. Our pigeons behaved exactly as we wanted them to, and so far as I am concerned, Project Pigeon should have been the end of the "average organism" in the study of behavior.

A second offshoot was theoretical. Near the end of the book I raised the question of whether human behavior had "properties . . . which will require a different kind of treatment [from that of nonhuman animals]?" I thought we could not answer that question so long as we knew so little about either kind, but "the only differences I expect to see . . . between the behavior of rat and man (aside from enormous differences of complexity) lie in the field of verbal behavior." I had begun writing a book on that subject before finishing *The Behavior of Organisms*, and I returned to it on a Guggenheim fellowship when the Manhattan Project made the precision bombing of Project Pigeon unnecessary. *Verbal Behavior* was not published until 1957, but in 1945 I was asked to contribute to a symposium on operationism, and I took some material from the manuscript. How do we learn to talk about private events? Most of the first paragraph of Watson's manifesto was an attack on introspection. Data obtained through introspection, said Watson, were not "objective" and could not be used in a natural science. That was an anticipation of logical positivism, but I disagreed with Watson's distinction between objective and subjective. It was not, I thought, a difference in nature, character, or quality of the data, or even of their accessibility. It was a difference in the way in which verbal behavior could be brought under the control of private events. What one felt or introspected was not a "feeling" or a "thought" but a state of one's body, and one came to talk about it only under certain verbal contingencies of reinforcement. Introspection would always be a problem because the contingencies were necessarily defective.

A third by-product of *The Behavior of Organisms* was still further from a laboratory science. Within a day after finishing my paper on the operational analysis of psychological terms, I started to write the book which became *Walden Two*. The war was coming to an end; many people would be reconstructing a way of life. Why not make it a better way with the help of a science of behavior? Much of the book was a fictional anticipation of what was eventually known as applied behavior analysis. The book's protagonist called it "behavioral engineering." There were examples of respondent conditioning and, especially, the step-by-step shaping of operant behavior. Walden Two was a social environment or culture free of the negative reinforcers of governments and religions and the contrived positive reinforcers of capitalistic enterprises. It was free, also, of many annoyances of daily life that were due to accidental or careless planning. The result was the "good life."

The schools in Walden Two were not much of a contribution to the good life. They could have been designed by John Dewey. When my own children went to school, however, I became interested in education, and the special power of immediate conditioned reinforcers and the possibility of shaping complex behavior with a program of small, carefully arranged steps could simply not be overlooked. Good contingencies of instruction were beyond the reach of the classroom teacher who must teach 20 or 30 students at the same time. Like other professions, education must turn to instruments.

My first teaching machines were designed, like Sidney Pressey's, simply to reinforce behavior immediately, but the machine I demonstrated in 1954 used programmed material. IBM made an improved model of it three years later. It was a mechanical anticipation of the computer used as a teaching machine. Programmed instruction has become an important part of industrial and technical education, but the educational establishment is unfortunately still not aware of what it means to teach, and its burgeoning problems remain unsolved.

I have not yet mentioned the most important by-product of *The Behavior of Organisms*—the work done by others using the same procedures according to much the same analysis. The procedures have, in fact, been greatly improved, and experiments in laboratories throughout the world have yielded a vast corpus of facts beside which those reported in my book are miniscule. Not only are there many new facts, but, as in other fields of science, the facts hang together. They compose, it seems to me, the most consistent picture of what behavior really is.

That the majority of psychologists are not familiar with that picture is a fact with respect to which a 50th anniversary has another significance. Operant conditioners are said to be insular. They read each other's papers and books, but few of those written by other psychologists. That favor is reciprocated. The trouble may have its roots in history. In the early days of the experimental analysis of behavior, the editors of the standard journals would not publish reports of research on single organisms or with behavior recorded in cumulative curves. It was necessary to start a new journal, which has never been widely read outside the field. Similar difficulties in finding space for meetings led to the founding of Division 25 of the American Psychological Association. Its meetings are attended almost exclusively by behavior analysts.

The insularity has been costly. A recent paper in *Science* by Roger Shepard shows the problem. It is called "Toward a Universal Law of Generalization for Psychological Science." It begins with the classic experiment by Guttman and Kalish (1956) on stimulus generalization, one of the most beautiful examples of a behavioral analysis. In an experiment with pigeons, Guttman and Kalish reinforced pecking a blue-green disk on a variable-interval schedule. During extinction they changed the color of the disk at random across the spectrum. The numbers of responses made to different colors yielded the curve in which Shepard is interested. He then cites presumably similar data from experiments by cognitive psychologists, in which the errors made in memorizing invented names of colors seemed to show a similar effect. But what about all the other experiments that have been based on Guttman and Kalish? Instead of reinforcing responses to blue-green, begin with a discrimination. Reinforce responses to blue-green but not to blue. The peak of the generalization gradient will then shift toward yellow. Is the pigeon avoiding the color to which responses were extinguished? Not at all. A negative generalization gradient must be taken into account. It suppresses responses to blue-green more than to yellow, with the result that more responses are made to yellow, which is now at the peak of the curve. If the discrimination has been formed errorlessly, however, with the procedure designed by Herbert Terrace in which no responses are extinguished, there is no negative gradient and no peak shift. These facts are quite out of reach of any current cognitive procedure, and they tell us much more about what should be covered by a "universal law of generalization."

Forty years have passed since *Walden Two* was published, and the meaning of the good life has undergone drastic change. It is not enough to design a way of life in which everyone will be happy. We must design one that will make it possible for generations as yet unborn to live a happy life. That was the point of my book *Beyond Freedom and Dignity*, which is, I believe, another by-product of *The Behavior of Organisms*. How are we to stop exhausting our resources, polluting the environment, and bearing too many children, and how are we to prevent nuclear holocaust? How, in short, are we to take the future of the world into account? Natural contingencies of reinforcement will not do it, nor will contingencies maintained by governments, religions, and capitalistic systems. We need surrogate contingencies of reinforcement under which people will behave as if the future were acting now. Can we design them and put them into effect? In a preface written for a new printing of *Beyond Freedom and Dignity,* I say that I am no longer sure, but I remain quite sure that if we ever do, it will be with the help of a psychology that is, as Watson put it, "a purely objective experimental branch of natural science."

◆ REFERENCES ◆

Bartlett, J. (Ed.). (1968). *Bartlett's familiar quotations*. Boston: Little, Brown.

Boakes, R. A. (1984). *From Darwin to behaviorism: Psychology and the minds of animals*. New York: Columbia University Press.

Bridgman, P. W. (1928). *The logic of modern physics*. New York: Macmillan.

Bridgman, P. W. (1959). *The way things are*. Cambridge, MA: Harvard University Press.

Cannon, W. B. (1929). *Bodily changes in pain, hunger, fear and rage*. New York: D. Appleton and Co.

Chomsky, N. (1980). *Rules and representations*. New York: Columbia University Press.

Garraty, J. A., & Gay, P. (Eds.). (1972). *Columbia history of the world*. New York: Harper & Row, Publishers.

Costanzo, M., Archer, D., Aronson, E., & Pettigrew, T. (1986). Energy conservation behavior: The difficult path from information to action. *American Psychologist, 41,* 521–528.

Estes, W. K., & Skinner, B. F. (1941). Some quantitative properties of anxiety. *Journal of Experimental Psychology, 29,* 390–400.

Griffin, D. R. (1984). Animal thinking. *American Scientist, 72,* 456–464.

Guttman, N., & Kalish, H. (1956). Discriminability and stimulus generalization. *Journal of Experimental Psychology, 51,* 79–88.

Holland, J. G., & Skinner, B. F. (1961). *The analysis of behavior.* New York: McGraw-Hill.

Hull, C. (1943). *Principles of behavior.* New York: Appleton-Century-Crofts.

Jennings, H. S. (1906). *The behavior of the lower organisms*. New York: Columbia University Press.

References

Konorski, J. A. & Miller, S. M. (1935). On two types of conditioned reflex. *Journal of General Psychology, 16,* 264–272.

Laird-Johnson, P. N. (1985, July 19). Review of Gerald Zuriff's *Behaviorism: A conceptual reconstruction. The London Times Literary Supplement.*

Loeb, J. (1900). *Comparative Physiology of the Brain and Comparative Psychology.* New York: Putnam.

Loeb, J. (1916). *The organism as a whole, from a physiochemical viewpoint.* New York: Putnam.

Lumsden, C. J., & Wilson, E. O. (1981). *Genes, mind, and culture: The co-evolutionary process.* Cambridge, MA: Harvard University Press.

Mach, E. (1915). *The science of mechanics: A critical and historical account of its development.* Chicago: Open Court.

Ogden, C. K., & Richards, I. A. (1923). *The Meaning of Meaning.* London: Longman.

Oxford English Dictionary. (1928). London: Oxford University Press.

Pauly, P. J. (1987). *Controlling life: Jacques Loeb and the engineering ideal in biology.* New York: Oxford University Press.

Pavlov, I. P. (1927). *Conditioned reflexes: The physiological activity of the cerebral cortex.* London: Oxford University Press.

Peterson, N. (1960). Control of behavior by presentation of an imprinted stimulus. *Science, 132,* 1395–1396.

Polanayi, M. (1960). *Personal knowledge.* Chicago: University of Chicago Press.

Pressey, S. J. (1932). A third and fourth contribution toward the coming "industrial revolution" in education. *School and Society, 36,* 934.

Restak, R. M. (1985, January 20). Inside the thinking animal. *New York Times Book Review,* Section 7.

Russell, B. (1927). *Philosophy.* New York: Norton.

Sherrington, C. S. (1906). *Integrative action of the nervous system.* New Haven, CT: Yale University Press.

Skeat, W. W. (1956). *An etymological dictionary of the English language.* Oxford: Clarendon Press.

Skinner, B. F. (1931). The concept of the reflex in the description of behavior. *Journal of Genetic Psychology, 5,* 427–458.

Skinner, B. F. (1935a). The generic nature of the concepts of stimulus and response. *Journal of General Psychology, 12,* 40–65.

Skinner, B. F. (1935b). Two types of conditioned reflex and a pseudo type: A reply to Konorski and Miller. *Journal of General Psychology, 16,* 272–279.

Skinner, B. F. (1938). *The behavior of organisms.* New York: Appleton-Century-Crofts.

Skinner, B. F. (1948). *Walden Two*. New York: Macmillan.

Skinner, B. F. (1951). How to teach animals. *Scientific American*. December, 26–29.

Skinner, B. F. (1953). *Science and human behavior*. New York: Macmillan.

Skinner, B. F. (1954). The science of learning and the art of teaching. *Harvard Educational Review, 24*, 86–97.

Skinner, B. F. (1957). *Verbal behavior*. New York: Appleton-Century-Crofts.

Skinner, B. F. (1968). *The technology of teaching*. New York: Appleton-Century-Crofts.

Skinner, B. F. (1969). *Contingencies of reinforcement: A theoretical analysis*. New York: Appleton-Century-Crofts.

Skinner, B. F. (1971). *Beyond freedom and dignity*. New York: Knopf.

Skinner, B. F. (1972). A lecture on "having a poem." In *Cumulative Record*, (3rd Ed.). New York: Appleton-Century-Crofts. 345–355.

Skinner, B. F. (1972). *Cumulative record—Selection of papers*. New York: Appleton-Century-Crofts.

Skinner, B. F. (1978). *Reflections on behaviorism and society*. Englewood Cliffs, NJ: Prentice-Hall.

Skinner, B. F. (1979). *The shaping of a behaviorist*. New York: Knopf.

Skinner, B. F. & Vaughan, M. (1983). *Enjoy Old Age*. New York: W. W. Norton.

Skinner, B. F. (1983). *A matter of consequences*. New York: Knopf.

Skinner, B. F. (1984). The evolution of behavior. *Journal for the Experimental Analysis of Behavior, 41*, 217–221.

Skinner, B. F. (1986). Programmed instruction revisited. *Phi Delta Kappan*. October, *68*, 103–110.

Skinner, B. F. (1987, May 8). Outlining a science of feeling. *The London Times Literary Supplement*.

Skinner, B. F. (1987). *Upon further reflection*. Englewood Cliffs, NJ: Prentice Hall.

Smith, L. D. (1987). *Behaviorism and logical positivism*. Stanford, CA: Stanford University Press.

Thorndike, E. L. (1898). Animal intelligence: an experimental study of associative processes in animals. *Psychological Review, Monograph Supplement, 2*, no. 8, 1, 16.

Vargas, J. S. (1986). Instructional design flaws in computer-assisted instruction. *Phi Delta Kappan*. June, *64*, 738.

Wade, N. (1982, April 30). Smart apes or dumb? *New York Times*.

Watson, J. B. (1913). Psychology as the behaviorist views it. *Psychological Review, 20*, 158–177.

Watson, J. B. (1925). *Behaviorism*. New York: W. W. Norton.

Webster's third new international dictionary (1981). Springfield, MA: Merriam-Webster.

Williams, R. (1976). *Keywords*. Glasgow: Fontana/Croom/Helm.

Zuriff, G. (1985). *Behaviorism: A conceptual reconstruction*. New York: Columbia University Press.

Index

Index